FAMILY BOUNDARIES

FAMILY BOUNDARIES

◆

THE INVENTION *of* NORMALITY

& DANGEROUSNESS

Caroline Knowles

broadview press

Canadian Cataloguing in Publication Data

Knowles, Caroline, 1954- .
    Family boundaries : the invention of normality and dangerousness

Includes bibliographical references.
ISBN 1-55111-108-X

1. Family violence. 2. Child welfare. 3. Family social work
4. Family - Government policy. I. Title.

HQ809.K56 1997   362.82'92   C96-932263-1

Broadview Press
Post Office Box 1243, Peterborough, Ontario, Canada K9J 7H5

in the United States of America:
3576 California Road, Orchard Park, NY 14127

in the United Kingdom:
B.R.A.D. Book Representation & Distribution Ltd.,
244A, London Road, Hadleigh, Essex SS7 2DE

Cover design by Anne Hodgetts
Book desisign by George Kirkpatrick

Broadview Press gratefully acknowledges the support of the Canada Council, the Ontario Arts Council, and the Ministry of Canadian Heritage.

PRINTED IN CANADA

To David, Jessica, William and Sophie.

ACKNOWLEDGEMENTS

I WOULD like to thank the members of the LaMarsh Centre for Violence and Conflict Resolution at York University, Ontario, who graciously hosted the visit during which I gathered much of the material for this book. I should also like to thank Michael Rustin and the University of East London for giving me time off from my teaching duties there. Thanks are also due to the Canadian High Commission in London who provided funding. The staff of many organizations have also been generous with their time and library resources: the Institute for the Prevention of Child Abuse in Toronto, the Family Violence Division of Health and Welfare Canada, and the Sick Children's Hospital, Toronto. I should like to thank Francine Robillard and Leanne Joanisse for help with research and bibliographies; and Michael Harrison and Barbara Conolly at Broadview Press for their support for this project. And finally, I would like to thank David Mofford and various others who have taken care of my family leaving me free to write about the family.

CONTENTS

PREFACE

Is it possible to teach the Sociology of the Family without boring students to death? This question comes from many years of teaching family, gender, and social stratification courses in various British and Canadian universities. The family is potentially the most engaging area of sociology. Its students bring with them a wealth of experience and insight gained as members of families. They already understand the delicate complexity of the family: its internal dynamics, its power relations, its subtle forms of regulation, its negotiations, its structural complexity, and its ceremonies are intimately familiar. Yet when we teach the family we ignore this implicit knowledge which students bring with them. Indeed, we require them to "unlearn" it and see the family instead in "sociological" terms. In teaching the family we stress sociological theories of how the family operates, theories of family structure, change, and diversity. In turning the family into an "area of sociology" we insist on certain formalistic and structural preoccupations which transform the family from one of the most interesting parts of sociology into one of the most boring. We simultaneously de-skill our students, silencing them as expert witnesses on how the modern family *actually* works from the inside. This book is a modest attempt to insert insider accounts of the family into its sociological study and to recast sociological enterprise so that it is enlivened by biography, autobiography, and individual testimony.

In the context of what we might broadly think of as a liberal individualism — in which we see the family as a private concern and as an expression of individual choices and preferences — it is easy to give the impression that the "family" can be any arrangement we want it to be. This impression is to some extent supported by contemporary sociology, which stresses the "social constructedness" of the family. This is the idea that there is nothing essential about the family, but that it is simply the result or outcome of the broader social processes which build it. This kind of dynamic approach which sees the family as flexible and in a constant state of change is helpful, but in the context of liberal individualism it can give the misleading (voluntarist) impression that we have more control over the family than, in fact, we have.

The family is to some extent a voluntary arrangement. It is contracted and organized in an infinite number of ways, but it is also highly scrutinized by networks of social agencies supervising health, social welfare, and education. These agencies place limitations on what forms the family may take. They administer the family in ways which place some strategic boundaries around what its members may and may not do, and which sanction some ways of behaving and discourage or even punish others. This idea that the family was an "administrative invention" of some sort became apparent in a piece of research I did in London, in the 1980s. I was interviewing social workers about their child protection work and how they made assessments about the extent to which a child was in danger in a family. The potential for dangerousness was then and is still one of the most pressing reasons for family scrutiny intervention and reform. But I discovered that social workers had great difficulty predicting the risk of dangerousness in family life. My fantasy that all children "at risk" were removed from their families turned out to be false, not just because risk was so difficult to predict, but because there were no viable alternatives once children were removed: group homes are notoriously difficult to live in, and foster care has high breakdown rates. As a sociologist, I was struck by the gap between popular cultural images of the family of the 1950s American television variety and some of the bizarre and precarious arrangements called "family" which child protection agencies sanctioned and tolerated. The family is not just highly diversified; it is the product of various forms of regulation and administration. These family forms are not about individual choice and preference, but they are about circumstances, human biographies, and notions of child rights — especially the right not to be beaten and molested.

The focus of my 1980s London study was black families, the ways in which they were "administered" by social workers, and the kinds of assumptions which were being made about blackness (Knowles 1990). In my eagerness to comment on race I neglected to follow up on what were equally evident social divisions in the ways in which families were perceived and treated: class and gender. The poor—and especially

those living on welfare — are the most likely to have their family conduct scrutinized for failure. Nor does scrutiny fall equally on all family members: mothers and not fathers are seen as key players in family
life and are co-opted in their attempts to reform families whose conduct oversteps certain boundaries.

In this book, then, I attempt to follow up on some unfinished business as well as to suggest some ways of recasting the family as a sociological project. It suggests that although the family is indeed a diverse
and dynamic living arrangement, it is also the product of various
administrative interventions by social agencies enforcing certain conceptions of children and child rights. The family is not a matter of individual preference but is shaped by various social and legal sanctions.
Understanding the family as a sociological enterprise is about understanding the impact of these agencies as well as understanding the family from insider accounts. In this book I seek to understand the family
through a delicate positioning of individual testimony and the antics of
external regulatory agencies. The book brings into focus the family as
an administrative invention and as a domain of individual experience,
and it explores the impact of some of the calculations made by social
agencies concerning gender and class.

Caroline Knowles
Montréal

INTRODUCTION

THE Sociology of the Family has to contend with what is in effect a deep-seated conviction which is widely held and not amenable to reason. This is the view that the family is some kind of primeval living arrangement rooted in human reproductive biology, and that is has always been and will remain in its current form. Sociology has countered these certainties about the family by arguing that the family as we know it is both historically recent and constantly changing. It has also argued that the family is a key social institution because of the part it plays in reproducing the main structures of societies. The family, it is argued, is responsible for "social reproduction." The mechanism for this reproduction is socialization — the processes by which we learn and internally absorb our society and its cultural software. Theories of social reproduction and socialization are central to thinking "sociologically" about the family. This kind of analysis raises an important question: if the family simply reproduces what is already in existence, then where do social forms come from in the first place? What are the mechanisms by which the social is generated and sustained?

This book is concerned with addressing this more challenging question. It conceptualizes the family as a social form with some definite conditions of production (rather than a place where the social domain is reproduced): conditions which can be described and discussed. It takes the view that the family is an infinitely varied set of living arrangements. These arrangements are "performed" through simple daily tasks and negotiations — who does what, when, and how — which are invested with meaning by those who perform them.

The family is also crucially generated through its engagement with key social agencies: education, health, and legal and social welfare agencies. The family is not entirely private, but is open to public scrutiny through these key agencies which help to form and transform family life. These social agencies do not directly intervene in all families, though they do have an impact on the ways in which all family life is conducted. This influence can be implicit and subtle. Agencies develop professional narratives — stories — about what the family is and how family life should be conducted. This kind of professional "expertise" is highly influential and liberally dispensed through counselling and various forms of psychological and psychiatric services. It is possible to trace the influence of these professional narratives in the stories people tell about themselves and their families.

Social agencies also exert a more direct influence on family life. But they need a reason to do this. One of the main reasons why they would intervene in family life today is to manage family dangerousness. Concerns about family dangerousness focus on the safety of children and the need to effect child protection. It is around child protection that boundaries as to what is acceptable family conduct are established and supervised by social agencies. Child protection agencies have a mandate to supervise, manage and ultimately remove children from dangerous family situations: they manage the boundaries of family life.

It is around these boundaries that (professional) narratives on the family are generated. These make explicit questions which otherwise remain implicit: What is the family? And what is it not? What are the boundaries of acceptable conduct in family life? How much physical violence and sexual activity is permissible within the family? At which point should the possibility of family life be removed? These delicate professional judgements are embedded in social agencies' stories of family life. Boundaries are about membership and exclusion (Anthias and Yuval-Davis 1992:2): they are the places where actual lives encounter the mythology of lives, where private conduct negotiates the requirements of public policy and the professional gaze of those charged with supervising children. Boundaries are where the family's narratives about itself encounter the powerful professional narratives of public agencies. Boundaries are about transition and transformation, about contestation and struggles to define and manage.

This book mines the "narrative interface" between the stories of public agencies and the stories of individuals recounting their experiences of family life. An analysis of professional agency narratives is interspersed with individual testimony. The analysis of agency narratives allows us to ask certain questions about the family: How is it conceptualized? What is it thought to consist of? How are the roles of mother, father, and child conceptualized? What are the tension points between these roles? And what counts as unacceptable conduct in these roles? Normally these questions remain unasked. They are not posed in some general sense of sociological description but in specific, boundary contexts, in which public agencies are making decisions about family life. These questions are raised around a particular combination of circumstances: the potential for family dangerousness. It is precisely around notions of "dangerousness" in family conduct that "normality" is staked out. Normality usually remains implicit, and is made so in narratives about dangerousness.

This book, then, reviews conceptions of family embedded in professional narratives organized by a concern about dangerousness. The main agencies involved in this kind of concern are child protection agencies, which draw upon the expertise of psychologists, psychiatrists, doctors, lawyers and so on. It is with such expert narratives that this book is concerned, for it is here that notions of the family are established. Although each nation state has its own ways of organizing child protection there is a good deal of sharing of expertise. Child protection in Canada, for example, draws routinely on American psychologists, doctors, and so on. Britain looks to what is happening on the other side of the Atlantic in dealing with child protection and dangerousness. Spectacular cases of child abuse — Mount Cashel, the cover-ups of the Irish Catholic Church, the concentration of sexual abuse cases in Cleveland in the northeast of England in 1987 — reverberate throughout the English-speaking world. Because of this interconnectedness this book will draw upon material from Britain, Canada, and the United States in making its analysis, with the understanding that these represent quite different political and social policy contexts.

This book conceptualizes the family as a nodal point in a web of professional and individual narratives concerning child safety. The family is a narrative sociological enterprise. Families' lives are lived and performed, but family lives are also regulated and bound by professional conceptions of childhood and child safety. The family is socially produced through the plethora of narratives which speculate about what it is, and what it should be. It is pointless to draw a distinction between lived families and narrated families; we can only know about the family from the many different kinds of stories which are told about it. This is an epistemological point: there is no "reality," only the representation of reality in stories. As sociologists get back to studying stories, there arises the possibility of an enlivened and engaged analysis of the family which speaks about both lives and the administration of lives, an analysis which is contextualized by the different kinds of power relations — interpersonal and agency — which constitute the family.

Chapter One

THINKING THEORETICALLY ABOUT THE FAMILY

IN this chapter I intend to discuss the key points making up the theoretical (conceptual) approach of this book. In doing this we will encounter other approaches to understanding the family around which I will develop a critique. In this way I hope both to establish the intellectual context for the book as a whole, and to give the reader an idea of how this approach to the family relates to others. It is thus possible to avoid the conventional text book "tour" through the available theories explaining the family — Functionalism, Marxism, Feminism, and so on — as these theoretical tours can be both tedious and abstract. I say that these theories are abstract because they are not usually linked with a particular field of study or its methodologies. Linking a theory with a definite piece of investigation, as this book does, makes it possible to get a clearer idea of how a particular theoretical approach is used to understand the family. Theory in sociology should be about ways of understanding what we see and study, and not a separate discipline as it is presented in "theory courses." This chapter does not have the apparent impartiality of a textbook theory tour either. It is an open attempt to convince the reader that seeing the family in a particular way has some definite advantages over other approaches.

This book approaches the family from the opposite direction to that taken by conventional family sociology textbooks. The sociological enterprise of understanding the family generally makes an appeal to a "norm" or a "general case" in discussing the family and its relationship to broader societal structures. For example, it is quite common for Marxists to think about the family in terms of its relationship to the overall working of a capitalist economy. Issues like family dangerousness are not part of a mainstream analysis of the family, but are usually tacked on as an aberrant or pathological (sick) manifestation of family — the family "gone wrong." Dangerousness only gets in to sociological accounts of the family in order to demonstrate a new flexibility in viewing the family as a diverse institution. But dangerousness is neither evidence of pathology nor is it one of a range of new family forms to be considered. To suggest either of these possibilities is to absorb dangerousness into the existing frameworks of family sociology. In this context dangerousness needs neither explaining or framing. It is a tool with which to excavate some of the boundaries erected around the family in the professional narratives through which it is managed.

In contrast to these attempts to explain or frame dangerousness, this book begins with what is admittedly a minority whose lives help define the boundaries of family life: families who come to the attention of health and social welfare agencies because of concerns about child safety. It is precisely this encounter at the boundaries of acceptability in family life which generates a narrative on normality and pathology. In establishing what the family cannot be allowed to be, agencies concerned with health, social welfare, and so on, articulate conceptions of what the family is and can be. These are not just idealized or abstract definitions of family; they have definite social consequences. They have a force in practice and legal sanction in the area of child protection, an issue which has become highly significant over the last thirty years. By examining the boundaries of the family we can understand some of the conditions which produce the family as it is today, rather than trying to establish a general relationship (because one does not exist) between the family and society as a whole.

The Significance of the Family

The family is a much discussed arrangement with a significance which extends well beyond sociology to social policy and moral philosophy, and to the very fabric of social life itself. The family is a focus for analysis, intervention, and commentary. Many different kinds of narratives

— psychological, social policy, legal, medical, moral, and popular — converge upon it and shape it into its present form. Each of these narratives has its own social, political and professional agendas, but the overarching result is to make the family one of the most highly pressured arrangements in contemporary society. Allow me to explain this a little further.

The family has long been seen as an index of the general health and well-being of society in a eugenic sense.[1] Eugenics was an early twentieth-century concern with the "racial stock" of the nation. It aimed at encouraging the breeding of the "fit" and discouraging the breeding of the "unfit," with attempts to limit fertility running from birth control to sterilization. The fit were the socially and economically successful; the unfit were an underclass of the feeble-minded, the criminal, the sick, and the poor. The creation of the Eugenics Society of Canada in 1930 was an attempt to see the nation's social problems in biological terms which stressed the importance of heredity in the creation of a healthy stock of people (McLaren 1990:17, 107). Indeed, eugenics was very much linked with the "social purity movement" in Canada, which was concerned with temperance, social reform, and moral and social hygiene (Valverde 1991:17-18). In more recent history the family was also linked with the production of social deviance, especially juvenile crime, as shown in Bowlby's *Forty-Four Juvenile Thieves: Their Characters and Home Life* (Riley 1983:97). Since the beginning of this century then, the family has become the focus for various attempts at population control and social engineering. A "fit" family (it was reasoned) produced "fit" citizens of a healthy nation able to compete with other nations. The health of the family was hence the key to collective prosperity.

Echoes of this way of thinking about the family are evident today. Moralistic right-wing crusades — of which there are many examples in Canadian, American and British politics — see divorce, illegitimacy, single parenthood, and abortion not as signs that the family is changing, but as signs of family (and hence social) decay. Robert Rector of the Heritage Foundation, an organization working behind the scenes with the American Congress reforming welfare policy, says:

Illegitimacy is the primary factor driving most other social problems, from school failure to unemployment to crime to emotional problems . . . if the illegitimacy problem is not solved, this society will collapse. (*Vancouver Sun*, 11 March 1995, p. A16)

In this kind of narrative single mothers are seen as the unworthy recipients of welfare cheques paid for by the hard-working and hence worthy taxpayer. Single mothers have become an icon of social and family failure, and the implicit narrative is a eugenic one: in financially supporting single mothers societies sustain the breeding of their less fit members, the producers of pathological and problematic family forms. Social justice at the end of the century is clearly about defending the rights of the (better off) tax payer against the (undeserving) poor. Certainly the mythic "mother on welfare" was one of the Ontario Conservative government's key targets in the 1995 welfare cuts. Lampooning this popular stereotype, a columnist in the *Toronto Star* (12 August 1995) writes:

She's the young woman who got pregnant in high school and just kept having babies to keep the welfare money rolling in. By now she has at least four children by different fathers. She lives in subsidized housing, gets subsidized day care and spend her days watching soap operas...

President Bill Clinton's efforts in the United States to cut welfare benefits from young mothers unless they stay at home and remain in school are a clear attempt to discipline young mothers by keeping them at home under parental authority:

We have to make it clear that a baby doesn't give you a right and won't give you the money to leave home and drop out of school. (*Guardian Weekly*, 12 May 1996, p. 16).

At face value these initiatives are about the need to cut welfare payments, but seen in their broader social and political context they are about the pivotal role of the family in sustaining a healthy and prosperous society.

The family in popular and social policy narratives still features as an investment in the future social fabric and hence our collective prosperity, just at it did at the beginning of the century in the context of eugenic thought. Because of its central social significance the family is constantly scrutinized for signs of decay and decline. In this sense it operates as a barometer of a more general social malaise. An entire spectrum of social failure and pathology (prostitution, crime, drug abuse, teen pregnancies, and so on) is laid at the family's door, making it one of the most highly socially invested arrangements of our time. As the reader will see in the chapters which follow, the kinds of family failure associated with child abuse are routinely linked with this same list of pathologies in professional narratives.

The Family in Sociology

The social significance of the family as the place where many narratives converge in the ways I have just described makes it not just "another topic in sociology" but a central focus for sociological analysis. The centrality of the family in sociology is doubly underlined by its popularity as a "menu item" in North American university undergraduate courses. With the popularity of the family as an item of intellectual consumption for undergraduates comes an extensive textbook production, a lucrative business which, of course, greatly adds to the existing narratives about the family. Both of these factors make it important to understand what textbook Family Sociology consists of. Before reviewing the sociology of the family through some of its textbooks, some contextualizing comments on contemporary sociology are in order.

First, sociology is a *discourse*.[2] It is a set of statements which comment on society in the sense in which de Certeau (1988:61) uses the term discourse to describe a set of narratives or stories which have a fixity as knowledge. *Meta-narrative* is an alternative term which could be used to describe sociology. A meta-narrative[3] is a discourse commenting on other discourses. But it is important to note that, in general, sociology does not present itself as a narrative, meta-narrative or discourse, rather it presents itself as authentic "knowledge" and not as opinion or as a story. However, sociology is *not* authentic knowledge with a privileged relationship to "reality"; it is a story of other stories — a meta-narrative or discourse. Moreover, it is a rhetorical and moralistic discourse with no privileged relationship to reality at all (Atkinson 1990). Sociology is concerned with the production of plausible accounts of what society is and how it works (Atkinson 1990:15-16).[4] In the production of plausible accounts sociology employs certain textual practices: the presentation of "evidence" in a particular way, especially the use of tables and statistics, and leading the reader to an "inevitable" conclusion. These are simply ways of managing the narrative, and are techniques which sociology shares with fiction. These textual practices are used in order to convince readers that sociology offers a kind of truth (Atkinson 1990:40). As Atkinson notes, sociology "needs to reproduce a recognizable world of concrete detail, but not appear to be a mere recapitulation of it" (Atkinson 1991:15). The way sociology achieves this is by establishing a distance between researcher and researched so that the sociologist becomes the impartial observer of "sociological reality."

If we see sociology as a discourse, any concern with scientificity, objectivity, and truth becomes redundant. The idea of the neutral observer recording social reality, and the distancing of the observer from the observed so as to eliminate bias, can be seen as **textual devices** used to persuade, rather than as a methodology producing scientific "facts." One of the advantages of seeing sociology as a discourse or meta-narrative is that we can ask critical questions about how it is organized or constructed. Another advantage is that the social investigator takes on a new relationship to her subject. Could it be that the impartial observer has a connection to what she is investigating? Do the choice of research fields and the approach to the subject have a resonance in the investigator's biography? Instead of protesting their impartiality, researchers now acknowledge and discuss their relationship to their research. Establishing the nature of this connection, and hence what the researcher brings to the investigation, has become an important dimension in the production of sociological texts. Whereas empirical sociology was concerned with establishing the authority of the text, today sociologists are more concerned with explaining how

they produced their texts. Liz Stanley's (1992) comments on the autobiographical nature of social research are significant here:

> ... I argue that the narratively structured auto/biographical
> accounts and analytically structured theoretical accounts are in
> fact highly similar; what follows in this section is thus to be read
> as analysis and theory, as much as description and narrative.
> (Stanley 1992:110)

Theory is thus really autobiography. Sociology as discourse and meta-narrative is reflexive: it reflects back on the sociologist who plays an important part in the production of sociological knowledge,[5] a part which she confesses rather than conceals.

What does this way of seeing sociology mean when it comes to understanding the family? It means we have to look at what kinds of sociological knowledge we produce. It means we have to reflect upon how and why we produce it. It also means that academic sociologists have to take some responsibility for their part in producing a sociology of the family. If we are not neutral observers and scribes, then what are we? What is our stake in our discipline? It means acknowledging that we are responsible for producing a certain kind of knowledge about the family. Academic sociologists are often asked to serve as "expert commentators" by the media on family issues. Television stations and news reporters regularly demand the answers to questions such as, "Is marriage going out of fashion?" "Are adolescents becoming more violent?", and so on. In this way sociologists respond to, sustain, or challenge ways of seeing the family which connect with popular culture. And these ways of seeing the family, as I shall argue throughout this book, have social consequences. We do not live outside of popular culture, but are very much a part of it, both through our lives and through our work.

Academic sociologists also teach students — a significant part of the next generation of North American citizens and families — courses on the sociology of the family. University sociology is hence where the family is conceptualized for a large segment of North American youth. And while it would be presumptuous to assume that students passively accept or live out the insights of lectures and textbooks on the family, it would also be a mistake to assume that this knowledge did not have some impact on the ways in which students see themselves, their families, and their communities. Sociologists have traditionally taken refuge in the belief that other disciplines more powerful than their own — law, social policy, psychiatry, medicine, and so on — are far more influential in generating notions of the family. And while it is true that these disciplines are often linked with the concrete practices of powerful social agencies — psychiatry, for example, has some fairly Draconian powers of detention — sociology also offers professional expertise when it comes to understanding the family.

The view that the sociologist is a powerless, neutral observer of society is not a sustainable position in contemporary sociological thought. Sociologists must now acknowledge their role in the production of a knowledge which leads us to see the family in a particular way. Intellectual activity has social implications.

What follows is a critical analysis of the family as it appears in mainstream North American sociology textbooks. This may be more influential than we think in shaping the modern family, albeit in some subtle and indirect ways. It is followed by an attempt to spell out some of the textual practices of the account of the family offered in this volume. I have argued that all texts are the outcome of certain textual practices which are open to investigation, commentary, and analysis. This text is no exception. Once the veil of neutrality is lifted we are obligated to come clean about the way we write sociology.

A critical review of the sociology of the family

Existing sociological literature on the family — through which the family is constructed as an area of knowledge — reflects the current, conceptually diverse state of North American sociology. In general this literature is surprisingly descriptive, empirical, ahistorical, and lacking in critical perspective. Family sociology, however, is not monolithic. What follows is an analysis of some of the key kinds of text which pass across the desk of a university teacher of the sociology of the family.

The textbook market in family sociology is dominated by large

American publishing houses. Crates of unsolicited glossy volumes in their ninth or tenth editions asking for adoption as course texts arrive in time for the start of the academic year. On closer inspection these glossy volumes take a "family life education" approach to family sociology (see Rice 1993, Strong and Devault 1992, Saxton 1993, for example). They contain advice on emotional issues, relationship improvements, sexually transmitted diseases, sexual dysfunction, falling in love, and family budgeting. They stress marriage and intimate relationships, even in their titles, and convey the sense that individual human happiness is tied up with the quality of intimate relationships of which marriage and family are privileged forms (Lauer and Lauer 1994). They offer for example, the insight that

> Marital satisfaction is maximized when couples achieve a balance of power that is acceptable to them. . . . Some prefer the traditional pattern of husband dominance, and others prefer an egalitarian relationship. . . . Exchange theorists suggest that satisfaction in marriage hinges on the perception of equity or fairness in exchanges, rather than on the existence of a particular power structure. (Rice 1993:315)

Their lack of analysis makes these texts rather poor sociology. But social analysis is not their objective. Given the practical nature of their approach and the context in which these texts operate, these are clearly "how to live" manuals being served up as hopeful templates to the next generation of North American families. What they offer is an implied proscriptive (moral) regulatory discourse on young relationships. This is the "wisdom" of mainstream North American fantasies of family life, offered as advice to curtail the diverse lifestyle possibilities available to youth. These texts contain a conservative political agenda which is being offered in universities across the continent, advertising itself as sociological knowledge. Family sociology is quite clearly a moral regulatory discourse.

Standard Canadian family texts (see, for example, Ward 1994, Ramu

1993, Ishwaran 1989) generally avoid the more explicit moral and regulatory messages. They concentrate instead on being theoretically "inclusive": reviewing the family in terms of the standard offerings of modern sociological perspectives such as political economy, functionalism, systems theory, developmental theory, and feminist approaches. While these texts offer a theory "menu" for the family, they are mostly rather abstract in that they rarely ground the theories they review in concrete research. Nor do they attempt to establish which theoretical paradigms are embedded in concrete social policy decisions relating to the family, such as changes in taxation, attempts to trace absent fathers or the impact of reproductive technologies. Because theories of the family are not concretely related to anything, students of the family are given no sense of the social and political implications of using one theoretical interpretation over another. On the contrary, students are given the impression that theoretical accounts of the family are a matter of choice or preference. But theoretical perspectives have real social and political outcomes in the ways in which we understand people's lives. Margrit Eichler (1988) recognizes this in taking a more concrete look at the family through social policy changes. Feminist perspectives, for example, bring into focus labour force participation by mothers of young children. Functionalist perspectives, on the other hand, frequently overlook this in favour of women's nurturing role in sustaining the family. Both theories have political implications. As feminists highlight the need for daycare provision, functionalists favour other priorities supporting women at home. Theory, in other words, needs to be re-politicized.

It is also important to recognize that different theoretical paradigms do not peacefully co-exist, as their presentation in family sociology textbooks as "options" implies. Theories offer radically different and contradictory ways of viewing the world. Take, for example, the conflict between Parsons and Bales' 1950s functionalist view of the family and feminist perspectives of family life. Parsons and Bales (1955) see the family as an institutionalized system in which men and women adopt functionally complementary roles so that women nurture and men are breadwinners. In this view of the family, young children have close, intimate relationships with their mothers but not with their

fathers: "...he [sic] tends to have a special relationship with one other
member of the family, his mother [on whom he becomes] fully dependent [by investing all of his emotional resources] (Parsons & Bales 1955:18-19).

From this perspective, family roles are suited both to (gendered) personalities and to the overall functioning of the family as a primary unit of socialization: "the most important of these roles... is the occupational role of the father... (Parsons & Bales 1955:19). The appropriate mate for the male breadwinner is the "proper" woman. A "proper" woman is,

> ...a mature woman [who] can love, sexually, only a man who takes his full place in the masculine world, above all its occupational aspect, and who takes responsibility for a family. (Parsons and Bales 1955:22)

This kind of analysis is hotly contested in feminist writing, which asserts the right of women to a life which is not defined by the emotional needs of children and the domestic requirements of men:

> With the large-scale entry of mothers into the labour force, we have clearly entered a new stage. While couples may be privatized in their social relations, when we look at the family from the perspective of children, there has been an opening up in quite an unparalleled manner in a direction which is quite opposite to any privatization trend.... Children are given into the care of strangers for significant portions of time. (Eichler 1988:327)

The views of Eichler and of Parsons and Bales are radically different and incompatible views of the family, and these do not co-exist as cosy either/or options as many family textbooks imply. Theories have contradictory social and political implications.

In stark contrast to the theoretical relativism I have just described, many of the more interesting accounts of contemporary issues and controversies which have an impact on the family — artificial reproduction, child abuse, and so on — avoid consideration of theoretical

perspectives altogether. While these texts contain a wealth of potentially interesting details, they generally follow a descriptive re-telling of
the empirical research of others, offering little critical analysis or commentary. Despite its provocative title, Gloria Bird and Michael
Sporakowski's (1994) *Taking Sides. Clashing Views on Controversial
Issues in Family and Personal Relationships* is part of this un-theorized
"issue" genre of family sociology texts. If theory texts don't grapple
with issues, and issues texts don't contextualize themselves theoretically, then theory remains disconnected from current issues, political
processes, and our interpretations of the world around us.

The cataloguing of diversity is now *de rigueur* in family sociology
texts. Yet very few texts pay attention to ethnic and cultural diversity,
which tends to be the least well developed dimension of diversity.
Ishwaran (1989) commendably attempts to deal with ethnic diversity
but, like others, does so in rather simplistic and stereotypical ways,
offering descriptions of "the Italian family" and "the Chinese family"
which do not do justice to the complexity of either. What these
accounts generally forget is the extent to which there are many different versions of the Chinese family or the Italian family. Unable to deal
with multi-conceptions of Italian-ness or Chinese-ness they flatten
diversity into stereotype. The "Chinese family" in North America, for
example, is highly fragmented and diverse. What it means to be
Chinese is hotly contested around class, location, and generation, but
this kind of diversity rarely features in the analysis.

Most accounts of family diversity deal with single-parent families,
reconstituted families, same-sex families and so on (Ward 1994). This
liberal eclecticism is a welcome departure from the restrictively defined
(functionalist) nuclear family types which have dominated family sociology for so long. But as with accounts of theory, decontextualized
family diversity also appears to be a matter of lifestyle preference.[6] But
diversity in family forms is only superficially about preference and
lifestyle: different family forms have different social and political consequences. We need to do more than just acknowledge that difference
exists; we need to understand how different family arrangements
encounter the "administrative" definitions of the family operated by
social agencies. The same-sex family, for example, may now be a per-

fectly standard family form in textbook sociology, but how does it fare in adoption, child custody or taxation arrangements? Viewed in this **administrative** context same-sex relationships are, indeed, personal choices. But they are personal choices which are severely socially disadvantaged as family forms. Same-sex couples fight for spousal pension benefits and protection under the Canadian Charter of Rights and Freedoms on a case-by-case basis (see the 1995 judgement of the Supreme Court of Canada, *Montreal Gazette*, 27 May 1995).

While there are many theoretically sophisticated and empirically rich accounts of family life, these are not necessarily seen as suitable texts for family sociology courses (see Bertaux and Thompson, *Between Generations. Family Models, Myths and Memories* (1993), for example). Bonnie Fox's (1988, 1993) two edited collections on the family manage to avoid many of the problems raised in my critique. These volumes convey a sense of the family as a complex set of processes with a definite history, rather than a "monument" to be described. Stacey's (1993) account of the fluidity and negotiation making up the postmodern family, and based on her research in Silicon Valley in the United States, discusses some of the intricacies of modern family life. Both the complexity and the diversity of the family in Canada is vividly portrayed in Bradbury's (1992) historical collection of essays comprising Bouchard's work on rural Quebec and Porter's work on Newfoundland. This work counters, with its picture of fragmentation and diversity, the mythology of family sociology which still largely subscribes to a "golden age" of traditionalism and community solidarity from which the modern family has fallen.

This book shares some of the theoretical ground established by the Fox and Bradbury collections and by Stacey's work on the postmodern family. All of these blend theory with empirical work and place the family in historical and social policy frameworks. This book also sees the family as socially produced: the outcome of certain ways of seeing and administering the family, ways which can be explored and discussed. The family is not just a place where the reproduction of society in its current form takes place, as most of the other texts reviewed imply. In this book the family is seen as generated through a number of mechanisms: through social agencies' and child experts' attempts to administer dangerous families, and through the ways in which individuals reflect upon their lives and give them meaning. We are concerned here with understanding the social and political forces embedded in the discourses and narratives through which the modern family is generated, with how these discourses and narratives operate through definite social apparatuses and administrations, and most especially those dealing with child abuse. The approach to the family in this book is explored below: not by reviewing a theoretical paradigm but by setting out a few of the key theoretical devices around which the book is structured.

Some Concepts for Understanding the Social Production of the Family

Some of the concepts drawn from the work of Foucault and Donzelot are particulary useful in situating the family theoretically. One of Foucault's biographers says of him that his "life was also the intellectual life of France. There are few changes that are not reflected in his work, and there are few developments that he did not influence (Macey 1993:xi). Developing the paradigmatic shifts of the French sociolinguists such as Roland Barthes and Ferdinand de Saussure, Foucault has changed the ways in which we think about social power. Donzelot, a student of Foucault and of Gilles Deleuze, documents the history of "the social" sphere and the ways in which social agencies — medicine, health, education, and so on — regulated and shaped the family in eighteenth- and nineteenth-century France. Although the historical details of the social organization of family regulation in North America are quite different from those of France, some of the concepts developed by Foucault and Donzelot can be effectively used to make an analysis of the family in North America.

Power

Power is a central concept in understanding how the family is socially produced and maintained. Guided by Foucault's and Donzelot's analyses of power, we may see the family as a set of socially mediated and socially generated outcomes shaped by power. That is, the family is the outcome of the exercise of power. But what is power? Foucault [31] (1977:102) addresses this by asking, "How is power exercised?" Or more specifically and helpfully for our purposes, "By what means is power exercised in specific domains or areas and under particular historical conditions?" (Cousins and Hussain 1984:228). Power concerns the strategies (techniques and actions) of various forms of social dominance (or hegemony) and is exercised through relationships, public and private, formal and informal (Foucault 1980:93). Power, in fact, "is everywhere; not because it embraces everything, but because it comes from everywhere" (Foucault 1980:93), and is "exercised from innumerable points" and "relationships" (Foucault 1980:94). We can develop this idea to suggest that power, in fact, is invested in everyday action and practices. Power is being exercised when a judge sentences a criminal, an obvious use of power. But power is also being exercised when the desks in a classroom are placed in a row and the professor stands at the front. Power is being exercised in labelling students "good" and "bad," "A students" and "B students." Power is being exercised when a mother silences a child with a raised eyebrow. Power is exercised through administrative procedures and in countless other ways.

Foucault's notion of power is decentred. It does not come from a central authority like the state or a capitalist economy as it does in a Marxist analysis; instead, power is highly dispersed. And this notion of power is particularly applicable to understanding the family. The family is generated, sustained, and shaped through the webs of power relationships which operate around and within it, and which regulate it in both subtle and obvious ways. These regulators can be very diverse: they can be laws which require children to go to school; school dress codes and requirements that parents supervise homework; neighbourhood participation in building a playground; or pressure from children on parents for greater autonomy. These are very different kinds of regulators ranging from legal statute to emotional pressure but they are all about the exercise of (non-equivalent) forms of power. In considering more systematically the nature of the power operating around and within the family, I draw from Foucault's analysis three key dimensions of power.

The first dimension is the power to name and to classify, to say what things are (Foucault 1977:194, 231). Developing Foucault's "power to name" idea makes it possible to ask a series of critical questions about the family. Which social arrangements are permitted to bear the name "family"? How is the family (differently) construed in the networks of administrative practices, laws and customs which hold the power to name it, to say what it is, and what it is not? What are the social boundaries which operate around the family? In what circumstances is there intervention to regulate or deny the right to family life?

The second dimension concerns the power to constitute subjects (Dreyfus and Rabinow 1983:208-9). The constitution of named and socially recognizable subjects — the sick, the insane, mothers, fathers, children and so on — are some of the outcomes of the exercise of power. Foucault's framework allows us to ask critical questions about how these social categories are construed. In this book I am particularly concerned with how mothers, fathers, and children are socially constituted as subjects through administrative processes. What is the range of meanings associated with these categories? What are their minimal requirements, and what are their ideal ones? And how are tension points between contested meanings managed? We can thus go beyond the descriptions of popular cultural meaning (family, mother, father and child) and look at meaning as it is put into practice in definite social practices like child protection. Using Foucault's notion of the "constitution of subjects" does, of course, require elaboration to make it useful in undertaking an analysis of something like child abuse. Foucault has been highly criticized for his lack of understanding of subjectivity (Rose 1989). Subjectivity refers to the world of the individual. It is a form of analysis which admits the significance of the internal personal world of the individual and his or her own life circumstances. Foucault has also been criticized by many feminists for failing to understand how subjectivity is gendered. Nor did Foucault appear to take account of the ways in which the individual's notions of the self encounter the regulations of social agencies. These problems with his framework give us reasons why it cannot be used on its own.

Finally, power is about the operation of networks of discipline and regulation around the family, which create and organize it in more or less subtle forms (Foucault 1977:209). Some of the techniques of social regulation are normalizing and moralizing judgement (Donzelot

1979:58-81), examination, surveillance, reform, correction, and assessment (Foucault 1977:172-194). These regulatory techniques can be
effective through all sorts of networks—formal and informal, public
and private—such as traditions within families, advertising notions of
lifestyle, demands made by school on the home, legal proscriptions
concerning adoption or marriage, peer group pressure, child protection
intervention by social welfare agencies, welfare regulations, medical
monitoring of pregnancy, and so on. These are just some of the networks which actively constitute family forms and regulate the spectrum
of acceptable conduct in family life. Foucault and Donzelot focus on
social agencies — medicine, social welfare work, psychiatry, the law,
and so on — which have a formal and publicly sanctioned mandate to
regulate family life. These networks are powerful precisely because they
carry the weight of public sanction. While power is dispersed and exists
everywhere, inside the family and out, not all forms of power are equiv-
alent.

Discipline and regulation

The family, then, may be seen as the product of disciplinary society. It
is a nodal point in a web of social practices and regulations which operate both within and around it. The family is both the outcome of disciplinary society, and a disciplinary force itself. But discipline and regulation are not abstractions; they have definite forms of social agency,
mostly in the form of the administrations of professionals charged
with supervising family conduct. Although Foucault (1983:224) concedes that the family generates itself internally and privately through
its internal networks, he focuses on its generation by the interventions
of outside agencies in the public domain. Internal family organization,
though not necessarily conceptualized as regulation, has been studied
by feminists who look at the gendered organization of housework and
work outside of the house, by sociologists who look at the distribution
of family finances, and by psychoanalysts who draw important clues
about the emotional interior of the family from their casework. The
public agencies of family discipline and regulation are extensively
explored in Foucault's *The History of Sexuality* (1980) and in

Donzelot's *Policing of Families* (1979). Here the agents of disciplinary society — education, health, social welfare, psychiatry, and the judiciary — play a significant part in generating and sustaining the modern family through their various modes of intervention and surveillance. It is the administrative actions of these kinds of agencies which feature most significantly in this volume.

The "tutelary complex"(1979:96-168) is Donzelot's term for the networks of public agencies, the regulatory apparatus, which screens family conduct for signs of "failure." The surveillance of family life is partly universalistic, as in the case of education and health agencies, which are in a good position to screen the conduct of all families. All children pass beneath the gaze of pediatricians and teachers, and in Canada this screening can be extensive. The day care centre attended by one of my children was visited by health inspectors who prised open lunch boxes, demanded ice-packs, and passed on some patronizing comments about nutrition to parents. The Protestant School Board of Greater Montreal sends an annual letter to parents setting out the "proper" contents of a child's school lunch box: no cookies unless they are homemade, only real juice, and so on. The government is definitely in our children's lunch boxes. It is also in our beds with frightening messages about the dangers of unprotected sex. Yet surveillance is not just about the activities of agencies; we also regulate one another's behaviour. Parents share what are effectively moral regulatory narratives on how to parent: these establish the boundaries of the possible and the impermissible in parenting behaviour. But agency surveillance is also selectively focused on those who most need to make claims upon public resources: the poor. It is the poor who are the most screened by psychiatric, correctional, and social welfare services. It is the poor whose lives are the most entangled in the administrations of complicated bureaucracies dispensing welfare cheques, food stamps, Medicaid, and subsidies for housing and day care places. The idea of the tutelary complex makes the point that family life is only a partially private domain. The family constantly erupts into public concern when the agencies of surveillance detect serious violations of certain norms and practices.

The forms of social regulation operated through the tutelary complex have, since the eighteenth century, primarily occurred around the management of children. Forms of regulation around sexuality, labour, and educational needs have, in turn, given meaning and substance to the concept of childhood (Donzelot 1979, Foucault 1980). This management of children exacts certain requirements of parents, and especially mothers, a point about which neither Donzelot nor Foucault makes a great deal. Both are more concerned with the overall social framework within which family regulation occurs. This is the more general disciplining of the population as a whole in the pursuit of social peace, and of productivity in the context of competition amongst nations for industrial and social progress. Disciplinarity, through which familialism was constructed around the needs of children, was ultimately about the broader project of the nation and its success against competitors.[7]

Analyses of the family using Foucault's framework

Although neither Foucault nor Donzelot develops an entirely satisfactory account of the family, their framework has been used most effectively to analyze it. Rose (1989), for example, shows how the organization, by psychology, of human subjectivity affects the normalisation and management of childhood and the ways in which parents see themselves. Carol Smart's (1992) collection of essays explores the construction of "women" as a category in legal and social welfare apparatuses, exploring the regulation involved in sexuality, marriage, and motherhood both theoretically and historically. Similarly, Riley (1983) explores the impact of developmental psychology and psychoanalysis on motherhood and the peculiar familialism of the 1950s.

These studies serve to make the point that although Foucault's work operated at a rather general, macro level — ignoring gender relations, subjectivity, identity, notions of self, and the internal disciplinary mechanisms of the family — his general framework lends itself well to a complex analysis of family as a social production. Foucault's analytic framework is much more comprehensive and complex in its conception of the family than, say, the Althusserian (1972) analysis, which rests on certain key sites associated directly with the state and its "ideological apparatus." Foucault facilitates the conceptualization of the family as a complex social product (Connell 1987:121) and not as a simple building block in which social relations are first encountered and rehearsed in preparation for the wider society, as the functionalist notion of socialization emphasizes.

Child abuse

This book is concerned with a particular range of private family practices which have, over the last thirty years, erupted as a public concern: child abuse. This is a concern which is dealt with by particular parts of the tutelary complex, notably the judiciary, health agencies, and social welfare and child protection agencies. Here we are most concerned with health and social welfare agencies who have a preventive, detective, and supervisory relationship to families where there is concern about child abuse and, therefore, child safety. Their interventions have generated a series of narratives produced by experts in the family, narratives which are centred on the meanings of the family itself, its dynamics, and the social roles of mother, father, and child. In fact, narratives concerning child abuse are where many notions of the family are generated in the late twentieth century. The need to understand what child abuse is, how it works, and how it can be managed has generated many expert narratives about what the family is and should be. The family as a social production is hence legitimately explored through the narratives, practices, and interventions organized around child abuse.

At this point it is worth making an important distinction which has a bearing on the production of sociological texts. This book makes an analysis of narratives concerning the family by agencies involved in either providing supervision or expertise (psychological, psychiatric, medical and social welfare) for those who perform the tasks of supervision. We are not here in the business of analyzing families as living forms in which people accomplish their lives, though this is undoubtedly what families are. This book is about understanding "representations" of the family in narrative form. It takes the view that we can only know about the family from the many different kinds of stories — professional, fictional, autobiographical, and so on — which are told about it. Narratives are hence the raw material which we investigate for knowledge about the family. This is a different kind of knowledge than we would gain if I were to follow a social worker conducting child protection work for six months. If I were to do this — though it raises many issues of ethics and privacy — I would be able to tell a different kind of story about the family. I would be able to comment on how families and social agencies concretely intersect in organizing family life. I would have a sense of how professional and administrative notions of the family narratives were performed (or adapted or ignored) by child protection workers. I would understand how scrutinized families deal with social agencies: how far they comply, protest or manipulate. But this is beyond the scope of the project in hand. I rely instead on the narratives of agencies and the expertise on which they draw. I rely on narratives setting out various kinds of expertise about family life and on the published biographies and autobiographies of those who have first-hand experience of family dangerousness. Neither approach is more "real" than the other; rather, both kinds of investigation produce different kinds of stories about the family. Even if I were to deal with live families rather than the family as the objects of narratives on the family, I would still be in the business of turning live families into narrative form. I would be doing this by interviewing them, and in interviewing I would be inviting them to render their own lives and experiences in narrative form. I would then render these into my own narrative about the family in writing a book about them.

The Family as a Narrative Enterprise

Narratives are simply stories, versions of events, people, and places. They are a kind of discourse, and like discourses, they "generate" social phenomena, so we can say that they are *constitutive*. But narratives (unlike discourses) are also *performative* in that people live their lives through them. Indeed, lives are the basic unit of analysis of the family, and lives are configured and reconfigured through narratives, in which people make sense of themselves and the world around them

(Ricoeur 1991). Lives are entangled in stories and can only be understood through the stories which we tell about them (Ricoeur 1991:31). This book is not so much about lives as the stories used to speak about lives — the *texts* of lives (Freeman 1993:7). These texts are partly the product of personal narratives; stories of the self. But stories of the self also encounter and negotiate the stories told by others.

The others' stories with which we are concerned here are the stories about the family told by social agencies concerned with health and social welfare and which screen family conduct for signs of failure. Agency stories are partly individual biographies of families of the sort which make up casework. These draw upon and generate what we may usefully think of as categorical narratives. These are stories which collectivize people, identifying social "types": the poor, women, single parents, and so on. Categorical narratives also draw upon the (grand) narratives of psychology and psychoanalysis thus constructing "types" in personality terms: needy, immature, overprotective, and so on. The stories of social agencies about the family in fact activate, develop and articulate narratives from a number of sources: popular thought, sociology, psychology, and psychoanalysis. It is these which provide the empirical material for this analysis of the family.

The family is therefore usefully conceptualized as a narrative enterprise in that a large number of diverse narratives converge upon it. These are narratives through which the family is understood and administered by a whole range of social agencies. So by examining some fragments of this narrative confluence we can understand something about the social construction of the family. But the stories we are examining are certain kinds of stories generated around the tension point of suspected dangerousness. Child abuse, our point of access to the family, is one of these tension points. So we are bracketing for discussion the family at the point at which it becomes an object of public scrutiny because of concerns over child safety. Denzin (1989:125) calls these tension-points "epiphanies": moments when personal pain and troubles become public issues.

But families also tell stories about themselves. There are family legends, origin stories, jokes, horror stories, colourful character stories, tales of great daring, participation in moments of public record like wars, and myths and mysteries and family tragedies. Family members are edited in and out of family stories depending on success, failure, notoriety, and so on. Blake Morrison's *And When Did You Last See Your Father* (1993), a moving memoir about his own father, makes an important point about the production of family stories. This extract hints at some of the ways in which family stories and told and re-told, edited so as to reveal some family members and conceal others. It comes from the kind of family gathering which occurs around the death of one of its members, a gathering which exposed Morrison to other accounts of his family beyond those he was used to hearing:

> Telescoped, edited, misremembered, my family's past seems a catalogue of grief and dispersal. But so many early deaths, and between the lines the other stories of alcoholism and madness and miscarriage and venereal disease and haemorrhage and mining disasters. . . . For my father to be facing death at seventy-five begins to seem, in such a family, not a tragedy of cut-shortness but a miracle of longevity. For him to have stuck it out with his children seems miraculous too, when the heritage is of neglect — children put on trains with address labels round their necks [a reference to the evacuation of children from British cities during the war] and pleading with their fathers, "At least come home before Christmas." And where were all the doctors and business men I had been led to think lay behind us? The talk here is of deck chair attendants in Blackpool, idlers of the dance hall or ice rink, chancers joining the U.S. Gold Rush. I'd have been cheated, once, to discover these departures from stolidity. But not today. It isn't just (just!) that my father is dying. Where he comes from is dying too. (Morrison 1993:41-2)

Understanding the family through some of the narratives of individual members gives the sociology of the family a more rounded and living form. Take, for example, a young girl's comments on her relationship with her father:

THINKING THEORETICALLY ABOUT THE FAMILY

Physically my father wasn't affectionate, but he said and did loving things, like leaving a book on my pillow that was pertinent to a talk we had. We talked all about my problems, from the practical daily ones, to emotional major life decisions. We went zillions of places together every weekend . . . he was relaxed, sometimes even funny on these excursions. I always liked him and respected him a lot, even though I feared making him angry or disappointing him — or worse, looking silly to him. (Hite 1994:181)

This statement gives the sense of a complex and nuanced relationship between father and daughter of the kind which is not possible from a more conventional sociological analysis of the family. In any case, the latter rarely deals with the quality of relationships between family members. In his 1989 autobiography in which he graphically explores the British prison system, Trevor Hercules says of his relationship with his (abandoning) mother:

I hated my mother for letting a young warrior who could have changed the world or been what he wanted to be suffer the shame of being unwanted, because even as a child you feel the lack of respect towards you, and you become very sensitive. Perhaps that's why in some respects I'm very cold now; but then again so are most people who have spent large parts of their lives in homes or institutions. There's no love there—just hardness. (Hercules 1989:17)

A sociology of the family which contains biography, autobiography, and individual testimony can connect with lives and experiences in a way in which more structural sociological concerns cannot.

Dorothy Smith (1987:167-8) illustrates the advantages of what she calls "institutional ethnography" which, seen through the lens of the researcher's autobiography, renders the everyday world as problematic:

I was for several years a "single parent." That concept for me provides a way of analyzing my biographical experience. That experience itself was situated in actual settings in which its mini-dramas went on — the home we lived in with its untidiness, the fruit trees, blackberries in the hedge between garden and lane, the view of the mountains from the kitchen window, the kitchen floor that would never come clean, the roads to and from the various schools my children attended. The children themselves as they were then are more difficult to re-envisage, overlaid as their images have been by their more recent being. I remember them playing soccer in the front yard and complicated games of fantasy in the back. In these fragmentary memories, there is no experience of being a single parent, though the work processes through which I engaged with those settings and relationships surely had that distinctive character because I was alone in charge of my children in a world of two-parent families. . . . It organizes and organized for me my relation to a school in the context of problems one of my children had in learning to read. . . . A child's problem in school, when it is made accountable in terms of the single parenthood of his or her mother, marshals procedures entering child, parent, teacher and school administration into courses of action specialized to this category of "problem."

In summing up the theoretical approach used in this book it is possible to say that the family is a particular kind of social production. It is the place where a multiplicity of narratives — personal, professional, and expert — converge. Hence, the family is not already "made"; it is "worked up" through various types of narratives (White 1991:150), and the stimulus in the generation of narratives is epiphanies. Power of different kinds and its effects in shaping the family are registered in narratives. And it is through the investigation of narratives that we can "know" something about the family.

Including personal narratives and stories of the self gives the examination of the family more existential ethnographic (Denzin 1989:131) dimensions. Personal narratives also provide a window onto what Connell (1987:121) calls the *emotional interior* of the family, much neglected in more traditional and empirical sociological enterprise:

The interior of the family is a scene of multi-layered relationships folded over on each other like geological strata. In no other institution are relationships so extended in time, so intensive in contact, so dense in their interweaving of economics, emotion, power and resistance.

A sociology of the family which is able to address its emotional interior will provide a richer and more engaging approach to the family. Indeed, it it explored in the (grand) narratives of psychoanalysis: Freud's discussions of Dora and of Screber, and Winnicott's *Piggle* provide clues to the family's interior, at least on a case study basis. So too does Laing and Esterton's (1964:33-34) phenomenological approach to the family as a site for radically differing interpretations of relationships and everyday life in the lives of schizophrenics. Biographies and autobiographies are also good sources of information. Moving in this direction of acknowledging autobiography as sociological theory, Dorothy Smith's (1987:167-170) autobiographical account of being a single working mother combines sociological analysis with experience, and brings into question the organization of the everyday world. The advantages of a sociology which addresses the emotional interior of the family are evident: it holds the key to a more complete understanding of power around the family than Foucault's, addressing as it does the subtle power relations and tensions within the family itself.

Conclusions

This chapter has critically examined the sociology of the family texts which are part of the production of knowledge about the family. It has suggested that sociology is a part of the intellectual production of the family as an object of analysis and that this has some definite social effects. It has also contextualized the family as generated by the disciplinary networks embedded in a multiplicity of actions and practices inside and outside of the family. It has suggested that we can know something about the family by examining the narratives which converge upon it. These are narratives generated around the professional practices of experts who supervise family conduct, and narratives which come from within the family as individual testimony.

The potential for child abuse is a major contemporary reason for family supervision and unleashes many different kinds of narratives on family life. Abuse survivors are also major contributors to narratives about the experiential dimension of family life. Published accounts of survivors' testimony can be used to catch a glimpse of internal family dynamics, and provide a counterpoint to the professional narratives surrounding the administration of family dangerousness. And it is to the notion of dangerousness and child abuse that I turn in the next chapter.

Notes

1. McLaren (1990) provides an excellent discussion of the impact of eugenic thinking and social policy in a Canadian context. In a sense eugenics has a contemporary version with implicit rather than explicit biological overtones. Economic and commercial competition between nations (if not races, though nations are still partially conceived in racial terms) is an important contemporary theme replacing the sabre rattling of the cold war era with feats of Japanese competition.

2. Discourse in the sense in which Foucault uses it in the *Archeology of Knowledge* is about the arrangement of statements and the relationship between statements. Discourse is a field of statements which can be investigated for its arrangement of objects and concepts. In this book our concern with discourse is about procedures and practices embedded in statements as well as the construction of social categories — such as mother, father, and child. Discourse analysis provides a grid in which critical questions can be posed about generative social practices (Knowles 1992:11).

3. Meta or grand narratives are much like discourses, stories of stories, by which the foundations of the social domain are explained. A useful account of grand narratives is offered by J.M. Bernstein (1991:109) who refers to them as second order discourses which

account for first order concrete practices which make up the fabric of social life.

4.   Atkinson (1990) argues that sociological writing operates through the techniques of persuasion rather than factual incontestability using the evocation of familiar cultural forms as a key device in narration.

5.   See also Liz Stanley's (1993) "On Auto/Biography in Sociology" in *Sociology*, vol. 27, no. 1, pp.41-52.

6.   See "Famille à la carte," *L'Actualité*, July 1994, for a popular version of this approach.

7.   Familialism is used by a number of authors to refer to the hegemony of the nuclear, two-parent family form in which there is an economically active father and domestically oriented mother which became an important cultural image in the 1950s. While this family form captured public imagery it can be seen as historically a specific and brief phenomenon, possible only among certain classes in high wage economies when male wages were high in relative terms and capable of supporting a family. The majority of women the world over have always been involved in economically productive work.

DANGEROUSNESS & CHILD ABUSE

OUR point of access to the family is the proposition that family life is bounded by the prospect of certain forms of dangerousness directed toward children. But understanding child abuse sociologically is no straightforward matter. Child abuse is situated at a confluence of narratives concerning its meaning; its significance to society; its legal, procedural, and administrative apparatuses; its agencies; its child expertise; its epidemiology (distribution); its notions of risk, prevention, and prediction; its social maps of dangerousness; and its concern with the psychopathology of dangerous people. This chapter discusses some of these issues because they have important implications for our later consideration of the social construction of "family roles" in potentially dangerous families. This chapter, then, is an attempt to say what child abuse is, in a way which allows the kind of analysis of the family which was outlined in the last chapter: the proposition that the family is shaped through its encounter with child abuse.

Child abuse is contextualized in a series of narratives about different forms of family dangerousness. In these narratives the family has an ambiguous relationship to dangerousness. It is seen in contradictory terms as both a prime source of danger and a refuge from the dangerousness of the wider society. The tensions between these two general conceptions of the family are played out in the narratives around child abuse. But family dangerousness is a more general issue than just concern about child abuse; it encompasses a whole range of violent behaviours, prompting an important theoretical re-positioning of the family at the interface between safety and danger.

The Family as Refuge

The family as the private refuge from the dangers posed by public spaces is one of the dominant popular cultural images of our time. As an object of popular narrative enterprise, the family is often coupled with the comforting metaphors of "home" and safety, denoting domains of individual control, choice, and personal freedom. Indeed, North American consumer culture presumes, and in its own way sustains, this cosy imagery. Danger in this interpretation is that which lies outside of the family and which threatens to invade and violate the bodies and property of its private spaces. Danger lurks on the street in many forms, especially crime and drugs, offering adolescents alternatives to (safe) family lifestyles.

Dangerousness as societal and external to the family is also importantly sustained in sociological narratives, most notably in the classic Parsonian functionalist conceptions of family, where its role in securing safety and social equilibrium through gender complementarity is etched out. The narratives of developmental psychology pursue this theme in their own way, connecting the quality of family life, and especially mother/infant relationships, with the quality of society as a whole. In this formulation the family "inside" is not counterpoised to society "outside" but bears an important responsibility for the quality of the social fabric itself. The old postulate that a strong and stable family is the basis of the "good" society is still a widely defended popular and intellectual position.

Child abuse seriously challenges the "family as refuge" thesis because it implicates parents as perpetrators of violent, uncaring, or sexually predatory acts directed at children in the social spaces where nurturing is supposed to occur. Of course, children are abused outside their homes too. Concern over ritual and sexual abuse has often implicated day care centres, schools, and even residential facilities run by the church (Baker 1988:5). The most famous of these incidents in Canada took place at the Mount Cashel Boys' Home in Newfoundland where several members of a Catholic lay order were convicted of sexual abuse; equally notable is the public apology (in 1992) by the Canadian Conference of Catholic Bishops to Native people abused in the resi-

dential school system (Begin 1992:14-15). Similar scandals have rever-
berated through the Catholic Church in Ireland, too, and have played a
part in the rapid secularization of Irish society. Jon Snow (*Guardian
Weekly*, 16 June 1996) details the extent of official "cover-ups" surrounding British paedophile rings which prey on boys taken into local
authority care. Abuse in the home is replaced by abuse in substitute
homes, implicating the local establishment of social workers, police,
and even prominent national figures, who are either directly involved or
help conceal the truth. Snow argues that the sexual abuse of children
has been given sanctuary in British society in institutions ranging from
its famous private schools to the Catholic and Anglican Churches.

In these cases of abuse outside the family the entire family and community, and not just the child, is cast in the role of victim. Resulting
efforts to enhance parental vigilance in defending children from the
dangers of the public domain enhances the status of the family as
refuge. This thinking is particularly evident in the "Stranger Danger"
campaigns run by many British and North American schools in which
children are alerted to danger outside of the home.

Webber's (1991) account of Canadian street kids nicely negotiates the
home danger/street danger distinction by showing that street children
(who are part of the dangers of the street) are themselves the product of
dangerous homes. Telling the story of her life on the streets with drug
dealers, a young woman talks about the home from which she fled:

> "You can't do anything right you stupid bitch" my mother would
> holler at me while smacking me across the head with her open
> hand. "Stupid bitch" and "bad girl" were practically the only
> words she ever said to me. I don't remember her being that cruel
> when I was very little though. I remember her as a perfectionist,
> always putting on the dog, pretending to be someone special. . . .
> I was very happy to be going home (from foster care) to my father,
> a hard slogging (and hard drinking) transport truck driver.
> Although he had a violent temper and rough ways, he wasn't
> mean like my mother. We always had a special bond, my dad and
> me. Maybe our bond was part of the reason my mother hated me
> so much. (Webber 1991:65)

The Family as a Dangerous Place

Dangerousness is a concept which has gained wide social currency since the 1960s. Originally it was not specifically focused on the family, but developed in discourses on law and psychiatry (Parton & Parton 1989:60) in which it was tied to the psychopathology of the criminally insane (Dale *et al.* 1986:27) and most especially to the need for prediction. The public demand for predicting who will rape, murder, maim or molest on an ongoing basis has fallen on those with professional access to the "mind" — psychiatrists and psychologists. Reviewing the literature on prediction from the United States, Dale *et al.* (1986:27) conclude that "indicators of dangerousness are poor and un-refined." The instruments for measuring and predicting dangerousness may have more to do with assuaging public unease than with identifying who should be monitored or incarcerated.

The modern contextualization of the family as a dangerous place for women and children[1] owes much to the intellectual endeavour of feminist scholars concerned with family violence.

It was feminists who provided an important challenge to the cosy picture of the "family as a refuge" thesis rampant in popular imagery, in functionalist sociology, and in developmental psychology. But feminist analyses of family dangerousness have always been rather narrowly focused on spousal or domestic violence directed at women. The feminist silence around child abuse can only be explained by the muddiness it introduces into the gender dynamics sustaining the theory of patriarchy: the idea that society supports the power of men over women. When it comes to child abuse women are implicated not just as victims, as theories of patriarchy would have us believe, but also as perpetrators of neglect, violence, and sexual assault.

This was more than a theoretical oversight. The silence around child abuse meant that feminist politics, in Canada, in Britain and in the United States, passed up an important political battle. In its embarrassed silence around the unspoken issues of female violence, child neglect, and predatory sexual behaviour, feminist politics failed to take on the most serious challenge yet to the demand for women's autonomy and rights. Child abuse, which raised the public demand for the professional scrutiny and management of child care practices, was arguably the biggest invasion of female autonomy in the second half of this century. This scrutiny of women's mothering behaviour did not accidentally coincide with the resurgence of feminist politics in the sixties; it was, in effect, if not intention, a practical challenge to feminist politics. But it was a challenge that remained un-met because to take it up would have forced feminists to rethink the victim status of women in the politics of family violence. Essentialist (biologically oriented) notions of gender at that time in the 1960s made this kind of challenge difficult to deal with. Men and women belonged to different biological categories with permanently unequal social rights and access to power. To have admitted that women could be responsible for family violence directed at children was to blur these gender boundaries and the albeit limited political struggles they sustained.

The conceptualization of the family in social theory as a dangerous place from the late 1980s appears to have both incorporated feminist concerns about spousal violence, and extended these concerns to include child abuse as a significant dimension of family violence. In Canada, at least, family violence has become "officially" a unified social problem: "officially" because the major sponsors of this theory are federal and provincial governments which have in some cases spawned an extensive research and information-gathering (and therefore narrative-generating) apparatus. Because governments are authoritative and influential sources of narrative, dispensers of funding, and setters of political contexts and agendas, it is worth pausing to look at some of these narratives and discussing how they are constructed and what they imply about the family.

Government narratives on family dangerousness

Combining available homicide statistics with those on child abuse adds important support to the "family as dangerous place" thesis. Health Canada's (1993:4) presentation of the homicide statistics[2] suggests that between 1974 and 1987, 39 per cent of Canadian homicides (solved by the police) were domestic events in which women featured as victims. Between 1980 and 1989, 542 children under twelve were killed, predominantly (76%) by relatives. Two thirds of those accused of murdering a child were his or her parents, with an even split between mothers and fathers. Young children are particularly at risk: a third of child homicide victims are under one year old, and seventy per cent are under five, with male victims slightly outnumbering females (Health Canada 1993:5). A similar pattern of familial and familiar relationships can be seen in the sexual assault statistics. In 81 per cent of assaults the child knew the accused; in 48 per cent of cases the accused was a family member (Health Canada 1993:6).

There are two very important federal government reports on sexual abuse: the *Report of the Committee on Sexual Offenses Against Children and Youths* (1984), known as the Badgley Report, and the follow-up *Report of the Special Advisor to the Ministry of National Health and Welfare on Child Sexual Abuse in Canada, Reaching for Solutions* (1990), by Rix Rogers. These hint at some alarming rates of sexual abuse. Rogers (1990), in the introduction to his report, gives moving testimony of the extent to which he had become convinced of the pervasiveness of sexual abuse in Canada while conducting his official enquiry.

My life has been deeply marked by my experiences of the last two years as Special Advisor to the Minister of National Health and Welfare on the Issue of Child Sexual Abuse. I have been shocked by the anguish and pain of so many victims and adult survivors. I have also come to understand that this problem is so pervasive that any child could be a victim of sexual abuse, including my own children and grandchildren. (Report of the Special Advisor to the Minister of National Health and Welfare 1990:11).

The British Columbia Task Force on Family Violence (1992) gives similarly unquantified but no less alarming estimations of the extensiveness of sexual abuse.

This report is an account of pain and suffering in what should be the safest, gentlest, most loving parts of our lives. Family and sexual violence is a social problem of such staggering dimensions that it is often described in terms of a national crisis. It is like a war in which we can provide only triage services while the casualties mount up. Should we mourn the dead, save the wounded, or protect the young?

Unfortunately this is not overblown rhetoric. Some victims of family and sexual abuse do die. Many survivors are severely wounded, both physically and emotionally. And our children are among the targets for abuse. (Report of the British Columbia Task Force on Family Violence 1992:46).

Why are two levels of Canadian government so intent on lending official support to the conceptualization of the family as a dangerous place? This kind of official narrative is connected with government-funded apparatuses which, in turn, produce more narratives. The Family Violence Prevention Division of Health Canada, with its National Clearing House on Family Violence has struck a particular political chord by highlighting the need "to eliminate family violence from our society" (Health Canada 1993:18). The research funding which comes with this has generated a narrative-mountain of reports by practitioners and academics on the various dimensions of family dangerousness — child abuse, spousal violence, and elder abuse — especially emphasizing schemes for "prediction" and "prevention." These reports have made it possible to write this book, and they highlight the point that narratives are generated in specific contexts and in relation to political agendas.

Some Canadian provinces, also conceptualizing family violence as a unitary phenomenon with a number of dimensions in elder abuse, spousal abuse, child abuse, and so on, have instituted their own enquiries. The British Columbia Task Force on Family Violence (1992) is one of these, but while it supports the federal government's basic analysis of family violence, it challenges the implicit message of the glossy federal brochures in drawing attention to the lack of funds to secure basic child protection in British Columbia.[3] This serves to remind us that although narrative-mountains are good for indicating the administrative or even social significance of particular issues, they should never be confused with practical intervention.[4] While it is highly significant that different levels of Canadian government (unlike successive British governments) are prepared to take on such an important issue as family violence, we need to ask some probing questions about what concrete outcomes this brings about. Does it bring more or better child protection and women's shelters? Does it raise public awareness? Or does it just provide research funds to write yet another report? Does it secure the impression that something is being done in place of concrete changes?

Family dangerousness, it seems, is a large, officially organized, narrative enterprise, at least in the Canadian context. But how exactly does this official narrative enterprise conceptualize family violence? And what is its political agenda?

The dominant paradigm, shared by federal and provincial governments alike, is to conceptualize family violence as a unitary social problem with some simple, if elusive, causes. In this formulation spousal violence, the various forms of child abuse, elder abuse, and, sometimes, the abuse of people with disabilities, are all collapsed into an undifferentiated notion of family dangerousness. The British Columbia Task Force (1992:1) even throws "racism, ageism, sexism and homophobia" into the dangerousness equation. The rationale for this aggregation of issues is that they are all abuses of power by the powerful at the expense of the powerless.

> Family and sexual violence is an expression of the abuse of power. It is violence by the powerful in our society against the less powerful. Sexism, ageism, racism, homophobia, discrimination against people with disabilities, the colonization of aboriginal people, and an acceptance of violence as a way to assert control all play crucial roles in the organization of our society. The pervasiveness of family and sexual violence is supported by deep-rooted social attitudes and values. (Report of the British Columbia Task Force on Family Violence 1992:46)

This report then goes on to analyze the family violence problems of people with disabilities, of Aboriginal people, and of immigrants and refugees, as well as elder abuse, wife assault, and child abuse. The rationale for including all of these groups is that they share with women and children the disenfranchisement of the powerless. Power in this formulation is deeply embedded in the structure and organization of society, and almost exclusively in its gender dynamics. The multi-dimensions of family violence which make up dangerousness are hence all presented as being about the social power which men wield over women and children. This is an attractively simple, but severely limited, analysis which repeats the basic feminist formula guided by the theory of patriarchy, that men are allowed to be violent because they are powerful and women and children are victims of violence because they lack social power:

> It is no accident that most victims of family and sexual violence are women and children while most abusers are men. Men's violence against women is a result of a society that accords men more power than women, socializes men to be aggressive and women to be submissive, and encourages men's violence as part of their masculine role. (Report of the British Columbia Task Force on Family Violence 1992:46-7)

Rogers advances a similar position:

> One of the most disturbing discoveries for me has to do with the impact of underlying social attitudes and values related to male and female sexuality. More than I ever realized, these tend to condition males to be sexual predators and females to be sexual victims. Our patriarchal society has set the conditions for sexual assaults and harassment, including the sexual abuse of children. I am increasingly uncomfortable with the realization that such behaviour has for too long been tolerated in our society. In my opinion, one of the most significant tasks ahead of us is to make major changes in the underlying deeply rooted attitudes of sexism. (Report of the Special Advisor to the Minister of National Health and Welfare 1990:11)

In contrast to the conception of power developed by Foucault (and examined in the last chapter) as dispersed and exercised in a myriad of actions and relationships, this is a very simplistic conception of power as a zero-sum game. In these official narratives of dangerousness, either you have power by virtue of your social position, or you lack it for the same reasons.

These remarkably consistent government-sponsored narratives on family dangerousness are useful at the level of generating a social and political climate in which family violence can be taken seriously. They draw attention to an important set of social issues and lay claim to the resources with which to deal with it. Where they fall down is in their attempt to offer a serious social analysis of family violence. They collapse what are quite distinctive social categories, all of which occupy distinctive social positions and relationships to family dynamics. Adult women cannot really be equated with children in terms of social and family position; and the disabled are cross cut by important age, class and gender differences. Family and social power is much more finely textured than is suggested by the crude gender scripts of masculinity and femininity as representative of differential social power.

Collapsing diverse populations around a victimhood relationship to some generalized notion of power is not just theoretically problematic; it is also politically disabling. Women and children are not only victims, but are also active social agents who make decisions about their own lives. The insider accounts of women and children in abusive families quoted in the chapters which follow certainly suggest active forms of social management by individuals presumed by theories of patriarchy to be powerless. Also, specific forms of family violence have solutions and forms of political redress in their own right. The disabled, for example, face all sorts of specific problems by virtue of their disabilities. Aggregating them into some more general problematic of the gendered power relations of society as a whole removes the possibility of limited change through the adjustment of social policy and practice.

The political agenda of the Canadian government's approach is certainly driven by a particular kind of feminist influence. This is likely to be about the allocation of resources and better social awareness, both laudable aims. It is not, however, clear that this kind of approach — inflating the problem, as I shall argue later — is actually very helpful in

raising awareness. It may even antagonize. It might be helpful in creat-
ing the political pressure necessary to release public money, but funding is not an end in itself: it is a means to an end. The end in this case
is about social change, and this requires a better understanding of the
various forms of family violence, and the strategies which are likely to
be productive in challenging them. The only understanding offered by
the official analysis we have looked at is that society as a whole, and
male behaviour in particular, are problematic. While this may be true,
individual behaviour is notoriously difficult to change without the will
to change. So while these conclusions might be correct, they are not
particularly politically helpful insights.

The Social Significance of Child Abuse

Although consideration of child abuse is usefully contextualized by
dangerousness and family violence, it also has a distinctiveness. It consists of a particular range of violent family behaviour. It has its own
manifestations and significance as a social issue, its own legal and procedural apparatus in child protection, its own narratives of expertise,
its own forms of prediction and identification, and its own maps to the
social and the psycho-pathological.

Child abuse also has a special significance in popular, media, and
political narratives where it is often used in making a more general kind
of social analysis. Child abuse often operates as a vantage point from
which to stop and take stock of society as a whole. It offers graphic
illustration of a general social failure with its implied question: What
kind of a society allows this to happen? In this way child abuse is cast
as a barometer of a state of social health and moral decline. It acts as
a "kind of wish fulfilment enabling people to discover what they would
like to believe" about the current state of any society (Dingwall
1989:49, citing Blum). It gives us a reason to examine ourselves and our
society, and to express outrage and indignation at what we see as its
causes. It is presented as the inevitable outcome of patriarchal society
(Report of the Special Advisor to the Minister of National Health and
Welfare, 1990:17) and as an abuse of the socially dis-empowered by the
powerful (British Columbia Task Force 1992). It is here tied to a

[56] demand for social justice, but child abuse is claimed by many political agendas: feminism, child rights advocates, and those who bemoan the decline of family values and the quality of civilization itself.

As a political and legal issue child abuse touches on some fundamental and conflicting issues of human rights. The rights of children to a certain version of childhood, prescribed by "experts," may seriously conflict with the rights and autonomy of parents in the private conduct of their version of family life. This is not so in cases where serious damage is being inflicted on children and is proven or admitted — no one has the right to seriously damage someone else. But some delicate issues over the balancing of rights are raised where abuse is suspected but not proven, and where non-life-threatening levels of neglect or simply "inadequate" parenting are involved.

Child abuse also touches on some fundamental areas of family conduct. These areas concern standards of child care, the use of violence in interpersonal relationships, and the boundaries of "proper" sexual conduct in intimate relationships between parents and children. All of these things connect with the more general issue of the boundaries of acceptable family behaviour. And family behaviour forms part of the general culture of any society. These family, social, and cultural boundaries are always being re-negotiated. Forty years ago "smacking" children was considered part of "normal" discipline. Today the use of physical punishment is less acceptable and, in some countries, illegal. The struggle to define the moving boundaries of child abuse and distinguish it from the "normal" in family life is intimately connected with core social values and judgements about personal conduct. As Dingwall (1989:43) suggests, the "outcome of that struggle reflects the distribution of cultural power." Child abuse in this context, then, is about that which is designated, by whatever combination of social forces, "deviant and worthy of moral outrage" (Dingwall 1989:43). This, however, suggests that child abuse is a matter of social consensus — that we all agree what it is and what it is not. In general this may be the case, but there are many "grey areas" around child abuse which are unlikely to be matters of consensus. Physical discipline is one of these; sexual relationships between adults and older children are another.

As an issue of social and popular public concern, child abuse has a particular trajectory. Parts of Canada, in common with Britain and the United States, had some form of child protection in the form of agencies and legislation by the late nineteenth century (Ursel 1992:109-113). Child abuse really became a high-profile social issue in the 1960s. The "discovery" of child neglect and the "baby battering syndrome" emerged from the medical research of Helfer and Kempe in Denver, and their radiological discoveries of the late 1950s (Parton 1985:131). This early connection with medicine is maintained in the form of a privileged relationship in which medicine is believed to have diagnostic powers over child abuse. Parton (1985:134) argues that the "battered baby" of the 1960s was less a diagnostic than a political term designed to call the attention of the public and the medical profession to a very important issue. With the help of the media's more sensational exposure these discoveries focused public attention on child safety and standards of care in a way which had not happened before.

The late 1970s and 1980s brought revelations about sexual abuse, sometimes led into prominence by the confessions of adult "survivors." Sexual abuse is in many ways the most private form of abuse as it is often entangled in family secrets involving coercion, threats, guilt, self-blame, and promises of dire consequences for disclosure. This particular combination of its secretive nature and the legal requirements for performing what counts as "evidence" makes sexual abuse very difficult to "prove." Hence, the prevalence of sexual abuse is open to speculation, and this speculation can lead to alarm and "issue inflation" as we saw in the two federal government reports referred to earlier.

The 1980s also brought to public attention abuses of the more collective, mysterious, and exotic kinds. Ritual abuse and emotional abuse have remained poorly defined and understood. So too has Munchhausen's Syndrome by Proxy, in which parents (usually mothers) harm their children so that they develop mysterious medical conditions requiring investigation and intervention. I learned about this particular from of child abuse from some of the first-hand experiences re-told to me by social workers whose dissertations I was supervising at the

Tavistock Clinic in London in the late 1980s, and who had witnessed, with the use of hidden video cameras, mothers harming their children while they were in hospital beds.

Each of these forms of child abuse has its own specific practices. They each have their own particular "signs" or symptomatologies alerting professionals to their existence. They also each have their own psychological narratives attaching personality "types" to certain kinds of abusive behaviour. What they share in common are certain "social maps" identifying problematic populations. They also share a rationale for "opening up" the family to a new kind of public scrutiny. With the emergence of child abuse as a high profile social issue, the family can be seen in ways it has not been seen before. Certain forms of behaviour in family life can be re-contextualized and rendered objects of professional scrutiny.

How Extensive is Child Abuse?

Assessing the magnitude of child abuse as a social problem is fraught with accounting and conceptual difficulties. Clearly some kind of accounting process which aggregates what is reported as child abuse is an indispensable part of national, provincial, and municipal planning and resource allocation in any country. But certainly in Canada even a fairly rudimentary form of accounting is complicated by a lack of national, and in some cases by a lack of provincial, statistics (Government of Canada 1992:3). This is because not all provinces have centralized registries, although all except the Northwest Territories have mandatory reporting. Seventy-five separate government ministries—federal, provincial, and territorial—have some responsibility for child abuse (*Report of the Special Advisor on Child Sexual Abuse* 1990:13). In provinces without central registries the agencies dealing with child abuse at the local level compile their own statistics reflecting their own concerns, working practices, and notions of abuse. Anyway, registries are open to contention on human rights grounds, and have been challenged for stigmatizing alleged abusers and violating individual rights to privacy (Baker 1988, Bala 1987). These arguments about rights hinge on the difficulties involved in "proving" abuse, in part

because child testimony does not necessarily comply with traditional
standards of evidence accepted in courts.

Accounting is additionally problematic when we consider that different agencies and regions are unlikely to be counting the same things, since there are no agreed-upon definitions of what counts as child abuse. The police, doctors, therapists, psychologists, psychiatrists, and child protection workers have their own conceptions of child abuse and their own standards of evidence. They also have their own quite distinctive, professional concerns and ways of working with abusing families. Taken in this context, agency, regional, and especially international comparisons of child abuse rates are of limited use: child abuse is locally reported, negotiated, and dealt with. In any case, child abuse rates are about what gets "seen" and counted as child abuse. Even in small countries like Britain there are large regional discrepancies in child abuse rates, which are most likely linked with professional and public awareness of abuse and with inter-agency co-operation. Awareness and inter-agency co-operation are likely to be regionally quite uneven, as the 1988 "discovery" of 545 sexual abuse cases reported in a single county in the Cleveland area of northeastern Britain shows (Campbell 1988).[5]

Despite the complexities of counting child abuse and other forms of family violence, official federal and provincial government sources in Canada are convinced that it is a social problem of alarming proportions. In fact, many Canadian commentaries are organized to show dramatic increases in rates of child abuse. Bala (1987:5), an expert commentator on child abuse, uses the Ontario abuse register — which indicates the number of reported but not the number of substantiated cases[6] — to show that while there were only 372 cases of all kinds of abuse and two deaths in 1979, this had risen to 2,152 cases and nine deaths by 1986. Between 1979 and 1986 there were more than 9,000 reported cases of child abuse and 48 deaths in Ontario alone. British Columbia, on the other hand, records its investigations rather than its reported incidents of abuse. It also breaks incidents of abuse down into neglect, emotional, physical, and sexual abuse, and gives a total for 1989 of just over 24,000 (British Columbia Task Force on Family Violence 1992:133). Despite accounting difficulties, these figures indicate some significant political pressure to define child abuse as a key contemporary social problem demanding more resources.

Some of the most alarming estimates are generated by the key federal government reports and refer to sexual abuse. The Rix Rogers Report (Report of the Special Advisor on Child Sexual Abuse 1990:13), citing Badgley's (1984) data, which was based on a survey of two thousand adults, contends that a third of all males and a half of all females reported themselves to be the victim of at least one "unwanted sexual act." A similarly alarmist tone is adopted by the British Columbia Task Force and by Baker (1988), reporting also for the federal government:

> The vast amount of unreported child abuse makes estimating the extent of this problem very difficult . . . Although the true incidence of child abuse is unknown, there is overwhelming agreement that the abused child is likely to become an abusing parent. (Baker 1988:4-5)

If this threat of a "cycle" of "dysfunctional families" (with all of its implications for society as whole) were not alarming enough, Rogers (1990:9) moves on to suggest that "all children in Canada are at risk." No one, in fact, is safe: "not even my own children and grandchildren." Sexual abuse, then, is such a pervasive social problem that every Canadian home and family is potentially violated by it.

It is unlikely that this "growth" in child abuse is related to major changes in social practices and behaviour, which is certainly the implication of the narratives of the more alarmist commentators who predict either social collapse or rampant male power. The growth of child abuse in official reports is likely to be the product of a small sample size (2,000), and also of a rather broad definition of sexual abuse as "unwanted acts." Many of those giving individual testimony to official enquiries are "adult survivors" reconstructing their own childhoods. While these individual and painful reconstructions of past experience are very useful evidence, they are not a good way of "measuring" child abuse. A self-selected group "speaking out" can give a distorted impression of prevalence. This is especially so if they are encouraged to speak by a very broad definition of sexual abuse and if their experiences are not contextualized in time and place, but all presented as part of a "present" problem. Adult survivors of different ages paint a picture of quite different times. Child abuse rates are also the product of shifts in public awareness. They are the result of shifting boundaries around what is acceptable in personal conduct. They are the result of shifting conceptions of childhood and an increased awareness of child rights. They are the result of increased professional vigilance and of changing and hazardous accounting procedures. And they are the result of an increased willingness to subject the family to critical scrutiny.

The kind of "issue inflation" surrounding child abuse has a creditable political agenda in asserting the importance of a pressing social issue and calling for the funding necessary to deal with it. But "issue inflation" is also counterproductive. It is a transparent strategy which antagonizes as many as it convinces. Exaggeration also plays a part in trivializing what are very serious social concerns about the violation of children's bodies and rights.

What is Child Abuse?

This question can be answered on many levels. At one level child abuse is, as I have described it so far in this chapter, a broad social, political, and cultural issue invoking notions of family boundaries and personal conduct. But it also has more precise and practical dimensions. It is a practical matter of agency intervention. It is defined in the laws of the jurisdictions in which it occurs, and it has some definite procedural parameters for establishing the veracity of competing claims about whether or not is "real." Child abuse is the object of a multiplicity of narrative enterprises, practices, processes, and procedures. Great precision is required of the social and legal agencies charged with identifying and dealing with child abuse because there is much at stake in "getting it wrong" or even in "getting it right." Child abuse cannot be understood as a socially constructed concept without understanding the network of agencies, power strategies and narratives through which it is administered. These are issues to which we will return. Child abuse, then, is a matter of legal and agency adjudication as well as a broad social, political, and cultural issue.

In Canada each province has its own child protection apparatus (just as each state has in the United States), its own definition of a "child"[7] and its own definitions of "abuse." Within the provincial framework of responsible ministries there is variation by area and by agency. Local social welfare, health, and legal apparatuses pursue particular conceptions of child abuse in line with the procedures and practices of their own professions. Police, social workers, therapists, psychiatrists, psychologists, and doctors all have different priorities and ways of understanding family life and their own professional narratives about abusing families. There are strong grounds for suspicion that agencies operate under quite divergent conceptions of what child abuse consists of. Certainly, child protection workers claim that other agencies and the general public hold notions of child abuse which are at variance with their own; workloads and resources often mean that only the most serious cases attract active child protection intervention. What constitutes child abuse at moments of intervention, as opposed to in legal statute, in professional guidelines, and in professional narratives of family expertise, can only be known through detailed empirical research on the actions of front-line practitioners.

Even legal and procedural definitions of child abuse are both imprecise and socially contingent. The British Columbia Task Force offers some examples of physical, sexual, and emotional abuse and also of neglect from that province which illustrate this point about imprecision. Physical abuse is "any physical force or action which results in or may potentially result in a non-accidental injury to a child and which exceeds that which could be considered reasonable discipline" (Report of the British Columbia Task Force on Family Violence 1992:135). What constitutes "reasonable discipline" is a social question which assumes a level of shared values about methods of parenting and notions of childhood. Non-accidental injuries also have many gradations. The most illusive of all, emotional abuse, consists of "acts or omissions" likely to produce

> . . . long term and serious emotional disorder. This might include effects such as non-organic failure to thrive; developmental retardation; serious anxiety, depression or withdrawal; or serious

behavioral disturbance. (Report of the British Columbia Task
Force on Family Violence 1992:135)

These are very hard to detect and rely on another set of professional judgements made by doctors and mental health professionals.
Neglect is defined as a failure to "meet the physical, emotional or medical needs of a child" so that their health and development are endangered (Report of the British Columbia Task Force on Family Violence
1992:135). Neglect, like emotional abuse, is about practices with outcomes which are diagnosable by mental health and medical professionals. It hinges on the concept of "child needs" and measures determining appropriate levels of physical and emotional development. These,
too, are matters of professional judgement and expertise.

These kinds of procedural and legal definitions of child abuse generate a set of concepts which are open to wide-ranging interpretation.
These matters of interpretation then fall to the "experts" on children:
pediatricians, psychologists, psychiatrists, and child welfare workers.
These professionals operationalize in concrete terms what are otherwise rather abstract definitions. And so it is around these delicate professional judgements that we encounter practical notions of acceptability in family conduct. These delicate professional judgements are
discussed in the narratives of professional expertise surrounding child
abuse. They are based on research and on experience of working with
abusing families.

Agencies and Dangerousness

The range of agencies dealing with child abuse—including law enforcement agencies, judiciaries, mental health workers, hospitals and child
protection teams—all have different skills, approaches and areas of
responsibility. They be can usefully be divided in terms of their relationship to child protection.

The police and the judiciary operate statutory child protection, a
process involving an adversarial system in which conflicting narratives
of family life are arbitrated. The point is to determine which are "true"
and which are "false." Did a child sustain bruises because she fell or

because she was thrown by an angry parent? Was the child next door molested as she claims when her uncle denies it? Is a child left alone all day while the mother works to feed her children really neglected or being cared for under adverse circumstances? The judiciary, as the arbiter of the veracity of accounts of the family, ultimately decides which version of the family is "true." It has powers to remove children or to enforce the supervision of family life by therapists and child protection agencies. Judicial action depends heavily on the evidence provided by those with expertise in children, whose job it is to verify the stories told by children, or even to tell the story that the child cannot tell.

Social welfare or child protection agencies are brokers operating between the experts and the judiciary. They are also themselves "experts" in family life. Of all the agencies, child protection is the best positioned to see what goes on in the privacy of family homes. (Other professionals tend to work with clients in their own professional offices.) They are also the best positioned to gain a sense of how a family behaves over time. Child protection workers pursue and investigate suspicions of child abuse. Because they do this, they have an important role in testifying before courts, and in presenting some of the evidence around which the court makes a decision. They also implement court decisions and make finely tuned judgements about whether accusations and suspicions require further action. They are the most "front line" of the professionals involved. Child protection agencies rely on a well-honed instinct for knowing whether all is well within a family (Callahan 1993:68-73). But they also rely on the research and professional expertise of others. Social work training involves exposure to the professional narratives of psychologists, therapists, doctors and psychiatrists, all of whom have theories about families and about abuse.

Expert Narratives

Medicine, child welfare, psychology, and psychiatry are key players in the production of "expert" narratives on child abuse. While I examine fragments of these narratives in the three chapters which follow, I explore some of their features here, so as to comment on the overall organization of narratives concerning family dangerousness. Each agency has its own primary texts, a distinctive narrative focus, as well as its own intellectual output. Psychiatry and psychology read child behaviour to reveal inner states of mind for signs of damage and distress. Pediatric medicine reads the body for signs of damage and arrested development. And social work reads the family for signs of serious dysfunction in relationships. Each of these narratives draws upon the others for support and confirmation of its assessments.

Medicine

The narrative convergence of expertise around child abuse is dominated by medicine, which provides the framework through which child abuse is conceptualized, identified, and managed. The "disease model" dominates the conceptualization of child abuse, and comes from its "discovery" as a medical problem in the early work in Denver of Helfer and Kempe (Parton 1985:131). Such disease models are used as explanatory metaphors. Giaretto, in discussing the Santa Clara County (California) Child Sexual Abuse Treatment Program (1982:263), suggests that "parental incest in the nuclear family can be likened to terminal cancer in the individual." Sexual abuse operates as both cause and symptom of broader family "dysfunctional dynamics," and the idea that families can be treated for sexual abuse is itself drawn from medical thinking. The "incestuous" family also becomes a diagnostic category, identifying an underlying "pathology [which] resides primarily with the parent but manifests itself in the relationship with the child" (Parton 1985:132) and which can be "treated" with only limited success.

The formulation of child abuse as a disease has generated a demand for diagnostic certainty in the detection of dangerousness (Woodling *et al.* 1986; Herbert 1987). This is particularly the case with sexual abuse, where the signs are internal and ambiguous and where there is a demand for forensic evidence. Carol Herbert, the Co-Director of a Sexual Assault Assessment Project at the University of British Columbia, who draws on the knowledge of the Seattle Sexual Assault Centre, suggests that diagnosis where there is no disclosure relies on behavioral indicators — sexual acting-out as well as medical examination:

> As physician examiners' experience has increased, particularly with young children, there has been an increasing police demand for diagnostic interviews and examination of alleged sexual abuse victims. Increasing evidence indicates that videotaping the medical encounter can be useful in the investigative process. Verbatim transcripts of the medical interview have been used by the police and prosecutors in preparing for court, in confronting alleged perpetrators and obtaining guilty pleas, and in evidence at trial. (Herbert 1987:219)

The formulation of child abuse as a disease has also generated a demand for "treatment" programs and for "prevention" schemes. This classic medical formulation is evident across a range of narratives and practices. Sometimes treatments are offered in clinical settings such as the SCAN program at the Toronto Hospital for Sick Children. Treatment usually involves psychological, psychiatric or counselling types of intervention for victims or for perpetrators of abuse, because despite its identification as a pathology, there is no medical treatment for child abuse. The design and evaluation of treatment strategies also feature highly in a number of reports endorsed by the National Clearing House on Family Violence (Annual Report 1992/3:5) which list treatment as one of its concerns.

The idea of prevention,[8] like treatment, gives the impression that something can be done about child abuse. It has a great appeal, for clearly it would be better if we could stop child abuse occurring at all. Prevention is a term borrowed from public health narratives (Justice and Justice 1976), where it is used to discuss arresting the spread of diseases. Prevention features highly in local and federal approaches to child abuse and is especially well developed around perinatal medicine, something to which we will return in later chapters.

Despite its narrative dominance, medicine has nothing to offer by way of treatment, and only some very limited approaches to prevention. Its greatest success is with diagnosis, and even this is a hazardous

process which relies heavily on non-medical interpretations of family
life. The literature pursuing the medical diagnosis of child abuse is
legion: Challin and Lewittes (1988) cite over fifty studies relating to
Canada alone, with a much larger literature produced in the United
States. Diagnosis of sexual abuse was the object of enormous contro-
versy in the Cleveland abuse cases in northeastern Britain (Report of
the Inquiry into Child Abuse in Cleveland 1987). Reflecting on diagnosis, a consultant pediatrician (Wynn 1989:29), notes that physical
examination in sexual abuse cases at least has "been greatly overem-
phasized." Dr Mian, an expert in child abuse at the Toronto Sick
Children's Hospital, concurs with the general tentativeness about medical diagnosis. She suggests that 40 per cent of sexual abuse cases have
no physical signs from which the doctor can make a diagnosis. And
diagnosis is no less hazardous in cases of physical abuse and neglect:
there are many reasons why a child may have broken bones; there are
many reasons why a child may fail to thrive in accordance with growth
and developmental norms established in medical charts. Being under-
sized and damaged are not in themselves sufficient evidence from which
a diagnosis of child abuse can be determined.

Diagnosis, which provides "few quantitative measures," is an "art
rather than a science" (Eade 1981:3).[9] Some physicians go as far as to
admit that "the definition of what is medical is purely arbitrary. The
dysfunctional (dangerous) family issues are partly medical-psychiatric
and largely social" (Rae-Grant 1981:25). In fact, examining physicians
rely on disclosure (Leventhal, Fearn and Stashwick 1986:71-78). They
can corroborate or contest the stories told by children about their
abuse. But in the absence of disclosure it is hard to make a "diagnosis"
upon medical evidence alone such as bruising and tearing. Physicians
also rely upon behavioral and social indicators such as the parents'
ability to produce a plausible account of the injury. Medical evidence is
contextual, and its context is a narrative about the nature of family life
and the social positions of its members, themes to which we will return
in examining the social maps of dangerousness.

Child abuse is also conceptualized in psychiatric and psychological (grand) narratives, where it operates as a "gold mine of psychopathology" (Parton 1985:134). While child abuse does not itself constitute a diagnostic category in psychology and psychiatry as it does in medicine, it is closely associated with other pathologies such as post-traumatic stress response and dissociative disorders (McGregor 1988:16). Child abuse is also increasingly conceptualized as a provoking agent for a range of psychopathologies including eating disorders and substance abuse. It is also seen as the underlying cause of a range of "sociopathologies" including prostitution and sex offences (McGregor and Dutton 1988:1-5).

> To appreciate fully the prevalence of child sexual abuse in prostitutes in comparison with normal [sic] populations, it is important to consider the form . . . and timing of the abuse. Prostitutes' sexual experiences occur earlier in life and they tend to leave home at a younger age. . . . Research findings on the prevalence of child sexual abuse in populations which abuse alcohol and/or drugs varies considerably. The study with the strongest methodology suggests an incest rate of 44%, a high figure relative to the norm. The strong correlation between substance abuse and prostitution indicates a need for further research into this circular relationship and their respective links with child sexual abuse. (McGregor & Dutton 1988:3)[10]

A variety of psychometric techniques are brought to bear on the potentially dangerous family: the maternal support index, the parenting stress index, and the inventory of home stimulation (Adamakos 1986:465) are just some of the techniques used. Experts of the mind, like the experts of the body, are heavily involved in the reading of social contexts, though this is often denied by the scientific requirements of the professional knowledge systems in which they operate. Along with medicine, psychology is the expert narrative which is the most categorical about abusing families. Its ways of conceptualizing the family, often in stark terms as though there were "abusing" and "non-abusing" types, is bound up with the use of empirical and experimental method-ologies. Casting the family in these terms, however, has important, implications as we will see in the three chapters which follow.

Predicting and Identifying Dangerousness

Social agencies and child experts, like the ones just discussed, mobilize their expertise in the important business of predicting that child abuse will occur or identifying that it is already occurring. The social demand for a means to effectively identify abusers and predict who is likely to abuse is a reasonable one, and it is made all the more urgent by child deaths from non-accidental injuries. Bala's (1987) work on child abuse and neglect deaths in Ontario, for example, effectively made the case for prediction. So too did the deaths of Kim Ann Poppen in Ontario (1976) and Matthew Vaudreuil in British Columbia (1992), both of which were the subject of official inquiries documenting agency failure to identify and manage abuse effectively.[11] Much of the demand for pre-diction and identification of abuse in Britain — where the list of young victims is a long one — has been around similar examples of the trag-ic consequences of agency failure to manage parental violence. While this demand to predict dangerousness is a reasonable one, it is also a very difficult one for agencies to respond to effectively. Attempts at pre-diction have had some significant social consequences in the labelling and managing of specific populations. These social consequences are the subject of the rest of this chapter and also of the next three.

The social maps to dangerousness

The social demand to identify and predict the occurrence of child abuse within the private domain of family conduct has some important social implications. The narratives and practices of agencies which have expertise to contribute in meeting this social demand have had a major impact on how the family is seen and understood. Most significantly, at least in some professional narratives, the demand for prediction has led to the view that there are two kinds of families: those where there is a risk of dangerousness, and those which are benign or "normal", if only by default.

Dangerousness in psychological narratives is thought to have an epidemiology: a pattern of distribution which is unevenly organized between two apparently discrete populations — the dangerous and the normal. Schindler and Arkowitz's (1986) work, for example, uncritically compares differences in mother and child interactions between "abusive" (dangerous) and "non-abusive" (normal) families. These two populations are expected to show quite different rates and patterns of mother and child interaction. The checklists (Parton & Parton 1989:63) used by health workers and sometimes, Parton and Parton claim, child protection workers, to assess family dangerousness also assume this simplistic division of families. Professionals must decide which family belongs to which category: dangerous families are potential abusers; normal families are not.

This simplistic demarcation is also evident in some of the well-intentioned community prevention schemes operating in major Canadian cities' public health programs. An example is the "Families for Families" project, based on Helfer and Kempe's medical model of intervention in child abusing families. This project identifies what are variously referred to as "successful parents", "healthy families" or "community families" as the "normal" group. These are sent as role models into potentially dangerous families as part of a project of family reform (Shaffron and Baslaw 1980:22). How are families assigned to each group? What are the clues, the social maps, which are used in assigning families to one group or another? Are normality, dangerousness, and the boundary between the two such clear matters of public and professional consensus? Might not dangerousness have a range of meanings from the murderous to the simply maladaptive or neglectful as social workers recognize in their interactions with families? Narratives, perhaps, do not have the subtlety of practice. They also may not be entirely "believed" by professionals and hence will not necessarily guide their interventions. Perhaps these are models rather than descriptions of real families? Whatever the case, rendering families as objects of administrative action in these terms has important social consequences.

Who are the dangerous? Dangerousness is construed through a grid of social and psychological assumptions. These assumptions are textured by a number of themes which provide the social maps to dangerousness. Parental biographies have a privileged position in the narration of the psycho-social matrix of family dangerousness. Past abuse and the quality of past parenting relationships in the parent's biography are thought to be especially significant in indicating present abuse. Silva Sawula (1989), a social worker working in Thunder Bay, Ontario, makes just this point in a pamphlet sponsored by the Institute for the Prevention of Child Abuse:

Supportive, positive developmental experiences result in a mature, healthy personality, making this individual more capable of providing good parenting care, while those who lack this are ill-prepared to handle the stress and responsibilities associated with the parenting role. (Sawula 1989:n.p.)

Parents suspected of abuse hence become the narrators of two childhoods: their own and their child's. The story of their own childhood is re-told in their conduct as parents. In these stories the past holds the key to the truth of the present and to the future.

Low income is also one of the central maps to dangerousness. The Children's Services Division of the Ontario Ministry of Community and Social Services (1981:5), for example, sets out in its training program for front-line protection staff working in the Children's Aid societies the link between physical and psychological neglect and low-income families. Similar connections are made in a number of professional narratives concerned with the identification and prediction of child abuse. Ayoub *et al.*'s (1982:414-415) account of "at risk" families in Oklahoma describes them as having multiple problems, many of which result from "poor economic situation" and a "negative family history." These lead them to exhibit their "constellation of problems" to primary professionals.

In practice, the short-hand for poverty and its associated constellation of social pathologies is a family's entanglement in the social welfare system. Those whose lives are organized by welfare are presumed inadequate and dysfunctional in a whole range of ways. Association with welfare also acts as a self-referential system in that those whose lives are scrutinized for one thing are presumed the population most likely to require scrutiny for another. These are the inhabitants of Donzelot's (1979) "tutelary complex."

The social maps to dangerousness are also marked by racial indicators, although this is more explicit in American than in Canadian narratives, which steer away from explicit racialization.[12] Kotch and Park Thomas (1986:169), in a study of social factors associated with the substantiation of child abuse in North Carolina, point to race as a key indicator of family dangerousness. They insist that over 30 per cent of child abusing families were black, 47 per cent were from single parent households, and 28 per cent were unemployed. Blackness, like being on welfare, organizes a list of other social pathologies. Blackness also has multi-associations with dangerousness in narratives concerned with crime, drug use, mental health, and urban decay. It is closely associated with poverty and welfare, revealing the extent to which many black families are systematically excluded from adequate means of survival in white dominated societies.

Sometimes the social maps to dangerousness have more to do with the requirements and expectations of the agencies involved, than the socio-psychological characteristics of the populations being judged. Ayoub et al. (1982:414), for example, describe the "completely dysfunctional" family as the one which demonstrates a "complete non-compliance with treatment." Health and social welfare agencies are often suspicious of families who, for whatever reasons, fail to comply with investigation and intervention.

The social maps to dangerousness are suffused with discriminatory judgements which place in a poor light low-income families, welfare claimants, single parents, black families, and those who do not respond well to being investigated. These distinctions, which operate around class and race, single out certain families to be scrutinized for dangerousness. We know from this that not all families lead equally scruti-

nized lives, but that the lives of the poor are much more open to observation and intervention.

This bifurcation of families into two types — normal and dangerous — has to some extent attained a dominant position in child abuse narratives thanks to the interventions of psychologists and public health workers. It is, however, by no means uncontested. We have already seen that it is contested in official government narratives bent on inflating the extent of child abuse as a social problem in Canada and which suggest that all families are at risk. Ben-Tovim *et al.*'s (1988:23-4) discussion of research evidence concerning the sorts of families involved in sexual abuse reveals that abusing families are predominantly nuclear, with two parents and a range of skills and educational qualifications. In terms of psychological indicators of dangerousness, the Canadian psychologist, David Wolfe (1989:2), for example, is sceptical of the "distinct personality syndrome or disorder" located in early childhood and around which a psychopathology of dangerousness is constructed. According to Wolfe, abusive behaviour in families is more constructively seen to operate on a continuum from mild to extreme forms. Abuse is then potentially a problem in all families. Child protection workers, it has been pointed out to me, do not necessarily work with this kind of dangerous/normal intellectual currency. Their practical concerns are much more about degrees of functionality and dysfunctionality in the families they work with. They are concerned with whether children are getting "adequate" practical care at the level of hygiene, supervision, and nutrition. They necessarily live, professionally speaking, with a sense of risk as there is no way of being certain whether a child will be killed or maimed.

The normal family

The "normal" family is sometimes referred to directly, but mostly it has an implicit existence in the cracks between the psychosocial pathology of dangerousness. Here it is the unspoken standard against which dangerousness is staked out. It was suggested earlier, in the context of the discussion of dangerousness, that dangerousness and normality have a reciprocal relationship to each other. The normal family is what the dangerous family is not: it is not poor; it is not the object of welfare scrutiny; it is not a single-parent form; it is not black; and it has no psychopathology. The normal family is rarely directly considered. But we catch more explicit glimpses of it every now and then. We see it, for example, in the "family function rating scale" (Ayoub *et al.* 1982:414), which offers descriptive measures of family dysfunction in order to "identify and treat families at risk of maladaptive parenting." The family function rating scale ranges from the "fully functioning" to the "completely dysfunctional." It defines the normal family as the family with properly defined social roles, with proper boundaries and with an effective communication system. Normality is also about families being able to meet their own needs without outside help (from the social welfare system) and about being effective in the task of problem-solving, as Sawula's (1989) social work oriented account suggests.

Of course, no one who works with families or who lives in one (which covers just about everybody) believes that such a thing as the "normal" family exists. This includes social workers, judges, psychologists, physicians, and psychiatrists: the very professionals whose narratives construe the idea of normality. My point is that the normal family is an administrative invention, invented in the context of the need to identify abnormality, which requires a norm from which to deviate. Dangerousness needs normality; without it dangerousness does not exist and so cannot be discussed or managed. My point about normality is amplified when empirical research methodologies try to measure aspects of child abuse and prevention. Establishing a "problematic" population and measuring its behaviour requires the verification obtained by measuring the behaviour of a control group, which operates in bio-medical research frameworks as a norm highlighting the characteristics of the pathology being measured. The issue here is not whether social agencies or other human beings believe the normal family exists; the point is that normality was created as a way of identifying and managing dangerousness, and this administrative invention of the family has social consequences.

Conceptions of what child abuse consists of are quite different when they come from the inside of abusing families. Inside abusing families there are no issues of definition, prediction or veracity; there are feelings, survival and a great deal of pain. These feelings are sometimes confessed in books and to talk show hosts. The following extracts are taken from some of the published stories of adult survivor. They are not offered as "representative" of experiences of abuse, because they are particular and individual testimonies which tell a different story: a story which is not a professional or administrative rendering of abuse or of the family. These individual testimonies show a contrast with professional stories and demonstrate the contribution of individual testimony to a sociology of the family.

Here is the story of a homeless young mother-to-be, herself a product of the child welfare system, speaking about what it is like to be on the receiving-end of child protection services both as a child and as a mother.

So, why didn't I get my CAS (Children's aid Society) wardship extended so I could get through this pregnancy? Because they think I'm a lost cause and they refused to help me. I had a baby when I was fifteen and still in care. In order to take him from me — I refused to give him up voluntarily — they terminated my wardship. That meant I lost my allowance, lost my subsidized room, and was forced back on the street, where they could claim, and rightly so, that I couldn't be a fit mother. In other words they deliberately destabilized my situation in order to take my baby away from me...CAS records are like prison records; even if you change cities, workers manage to get your file and find out about your past misdemeanours. I'm paying for mine now by being forced to spend this pregnancy in the street panhandling. I'll be on some street corner when I go into labour....

My mother is a hooker and a heroin addict; my father is a bisexual I never met. But I did meet my step-father. I lived with him and my mother once, for six months when I was twelve. That

was when CAS apprehended me and stuck me in a foster family....
When I was twelve and staying with them, he kept me locked in a
bedroom with a cake pan to piss in and a pizza box to shit in —
literally, no exaggeration. His idea of kindness was giving me
marijuana when he let me out. (Maria's story in Webber
1991:151-2)

In Maria's story social workers rescue her as an abused and neglected
child, yet sabotage her attempts to become a mother.

The workings of the "system" which she sees as organizing her life
are a significant theme in her story. The "system" is also monolithic in
her experience, not divided into different narratives and professional
practices.

Charlotte Vale Allen's story, told in her autobiography *Daddy's Girl*
(1980), is that of a middle-class Canadian girl, the survivor of an incestuous relationship with her father. In telling her story she is reconstructing her childhood. In this extract her feelings of guilt and ambiguity about her closeness with her father are an important theme.

At the beginning, it was a very special, very secret game the two
of us played; hiding out from the others. I'd creep down the hall
to the big bedroom those two nights a week my mother was out
to play cards or at the bingo; down the hall to play the new game
with Daddy. (but)..I really was wrong to have this secret. Wrong
this thing no-one was ever supposed to find out about; wrong and
bad. After that I went about feeling jittery, bothered. Yet it was
good to be held, to feel warm and protected; to listen to his voice
croon huskily in my ear; words spilling out to fill the darkness. I
wished I could just stay that way for ever: being held, feeling
warm. (Allen 1980:59-60)

This story makes the point that incest is also about closeness and affection and not just about the violence and power which are commonly
thought to accompany this kind of sexual violation of children.

Sylvia Fraser's *My Father's House* (1987) identifies her father's sexual abuse in her early childhood spent in Hamilton, Ontario, as the

cause of her multiple personality disorder. She has clearly reconsidered
her childhood through some of the narratives of psychiatry.

> When the conflict caused by my sexual relationship with my
> father became too acute to bear, I created a secret accomplice for
> my daddy by splitting my personality in two. Thus somewhere
> around the age of seven, I acquired another self with memories
> and experiences separate from mine. . . . Even now I don't know
> the full truth of that other little girl I created to do the things I
> was too frightened, too ashamed, too repelled to do, the things
> my father made me do, the things I did to please him but which
> paid off with a precocious and dangerous power. Thus for me the
> usual childhood reality was reversed. Inside my own house,
> among the people I knew was where danger lay. The familiar had
> chosen to be treacherous, whereas the unfamiliar, the public, the
> unknown, the foreign, still contained the seeds of hope. (Fraser
> 1987:15-16)

This story also supports some of my comments earlier in this chapter
about the inversion of home/safety, public domain/danger thesis. It also
makes some incisive observations about power inside the family — the
peculiar power of the victim which is not a theme found in any official
government or professional narratives. This man, discussing his violent
childhood, supports the victim/perpetrator cycle of many professional
narratives which take past abuse as an indicator that someone will
abuse:

> I got hit quite a bit as a kid. The last time my father hit me I was
> 18 — he slugged me on the side of the head when I swore at him,
> and I swore I'd never hit a kid. But once I hit a kid it got harder
> to control myself from hitting again. (Hoff 1990:126)

Although a different picture of child abuse emerges from individual
testimonies there are points of convergence with administrative conceptions. This points to a two-way process of learning between professionals and their clients. First, professionals listen and use their clients

to learn about child abuse. Second, clients learn from professionals to think about their lives and their abuse in ways which go beyond experience. This was clearly the case with the woman with multiple personality disorder who had reconfigured her narrative under the influence of psychiatry. Professional narratives are used by people to make sense of their lives.

Conclusions

This chapter has offered some preliminary comments on some of the implications of conceptualizing the family as a dangerous place. It has suggested that child abuse is a specific kind of dangerousness which needs to be de-constructed in order to understand how it operates as a part of a network of power relationships. In pursuing a sociological analysis of abuse as dangerousness this chapter has looked at what child abuse might mean, its apparatuses, its agencies and their expert narratives, its social significance and the social maps to dangerousness involved in the business of risk prediction and identification.

This chapter has also looked at some of the narrative themes of individual testimonies by people who have lived in abusing families or abused themselves. It has pointed to some of the points of convergence and divergence between professional and personal narratives.

This discussion serves as context for the three chapters which follow, in which I consider further some of the social implications of child abuse in the social construction of childhood, motherhood, and fatherhood. In these chapters I will be pursuing the claim that child abuse has significantly transformed the ways in which the family is conceptualized.

1. Dangerousness in family life is not, of course, a new theme the nine-teenth century was full of references to the "dangerous classes" but dangerousness was newly formulated in a particular way at this point in narratives about child abuse.

2. Include manslaughter, murder and infanticide (Health Canada 1993). These murder statistics are those released by Statistics Canada in 1991. The statistics on sexual assaults are collected from individual police departments (Begin 1992:5-6)

3. This refers to the actual services designed to effect child protection and not just discussion of services.

4. An explosion of narratives is a political bid to raise the significance of an issue and should not be taken to mean that there is an increase in popular interest or in service provision.

5. See the Report of the Inquiry into Child Abuse in Cleveland (1988) and Beatrix Campbell's (1988) *Unofficial Secrets*.

6. Different provinces count incidents of child abuse differently. Some record reported incidents, some substantiated or investigated inci-dents, and this makes an enormous difference to the statistics.

7. Conceptions of child are dealt with in Chapter 3.

8. Prevention programs are usually community based initiatives and are sometimes run by volunteers like the Dating Violence Program run by the Red Cross in Vancouver and the parenting support groups run in many larger cities like "Parents Helping Parents" project in Toronto and the "Families for Families" project in Ottawa. The SCAN pro-gram is based on counselling and psychotherapeutic models though offered from a medical site by physicians with special skills.

9. Eade and Rae-Grant are both physicians working with child abuse, so their comments about its non-medical dimensions are especially interesting.

10. McGregor and Dutton's comments are based on a review of American and Canadian literature published in a pamphlet titled *Child Sexual Abuse Within Populations that Require Health Systems Intervention and What is Known About its Prevalence and Service*

Costs and published by the Family Violence Prevention Division of Health and Welfare Canada.

11. See Children's Aid Society of the City of Sarnia and County of Lambton (1982) Judicial Inquiry into the Care of Kim Ann Poppen. This child's mother was accused of causing her death and her father of failing to protect her. The circumstances surrounding Matthew Vaudreuil's killing by his mother are to be found in the Report of the Grove Inquiry into Child Protection in British Columbia commissioned by the British Columbia Ministry of Social Services (1995). Matthew Vaudreuil was the subject of multi-agency intervention from the time of his birth, yet he was still routinely abused and neglected. His death threw a spotlight on the working of B.C.'s child protection services. His was not a case of prediction or detection, however, as he was known all along to be at risk. His case is rather about the management of family dangerousness by agencies charged with its supervision.

12. The racial politics of family dangerousness are quite differently construed in Canada and the United States. In most Canadian government reports native and immigrant communities are earmarked for special attention, but blackness as such does not appear as a significant dimension of the narratives. Native families are conceptualized as especially dangerous places, but then native communities are discursively linked with a whole range of social pathologies (see the Northwest Territories Native Women's Association and Social Services Department 1989 for example). Much of the narrative linking native communities with social problems is a petition for resources, but such appeals can also be stigmatizing. In the United States debates about dysfunctionality, poverty, and welfare are highly racialized as they are, though in a different way, in Britain.

ADMINISTERING CHILDHOOD

WHAT is childhood? How is it socially constructed? Through what kinds of agencies, practices, narratives or networks is it organized? What does it mean? Or rather, because there is no single answer to this last question, what are some of the meanings which have become associated with the idea of childhood? What are the main points of disagreement or contention between these meanings? And what are the social implications of these meanings for the ways in which we see and deal with children? These are some of the questions to be addressed in this chapter. Childhood is not just a focus on children: it is a focus on the social, psychological, and domestic arrangements in which children are cared for and raised into adulthood. A *child* is a person legally defined in terms of age. *Childhood* is a theory of personhood which supports an edifice of needs and obligations attached to children.

Consideration of childhood in this chapter falls into two sections. In the first half of the chapter I review some of the ideas about childhood drawn from academic research and writing about children. This writing and research comes mainly from sociology, history, anthropology, psychoanalysis, and developmental psychology. It sets the stage for the second half of the chapter which is about conceptions of children embedded in professional narratives generated by the need to "administer" children in order to effect child protection. The two sets of narratives (academic and professional) are in fact interconnected. Professionals working with children both draw on and contribute to the stock of knowledge about what childhood is. They are not starting from scratch. The two genres of narratives are separated here only for the sake of clarity. I have chosen examples of academic narratives concerning childhood which seem to feature, directly or implicitly, in the professional narratives examined in the second half of the chapter.

My purpose here is not to explain childhood in abstract or general terms; rather, it is to examine it in a specific set of contexts, in which there is a social demand to deal with children over the issue of child abuse. The question "What is childhood?" is a question with a specific context. In this chapter we are looking at what constitutes childhood when it is rendered in intellectual and in administrative terms. My point is that in speaking about childhood so as to render children objects of child protection, childhood becomes something quite specific. But this "something quite specific" has not remained in its own context. Child abuse has irretrievably changed the ways in which we think about children, as the following anecdote illustrates. A commercial filmed for Greenpeace by Hollywood B-movie director Roger Corman showing a woman being cuddled and then beaten to death by a group of naked children, was dropped in a howl of protest. The point the director was trying to make was that "Mother Earth," once loved by her children, is now being destroyed by them. It was not that the commercial's symbolism was lost on its critics; as Greenpeace's director in the United Kingdom said, she was pulling the commercial because "Child abuse is an issue in this country and for this reason I would not run it" (*Observer* 30 June 1996).

The context of this protest was the withdrawal of another British commercial showing two children flirting, which raised objections on the grounds that it might encourage pedophilia. The point is that child abuse has raised public sensitivity to the representation of images of childhood.

The demand for child protection has most clearly placed the issue of childhood on the social agenda in many countries. Abuse has forced us to think about the boundaries between what childhood can and cannot be allowed to be. The social demand to identify and deal with child abuse has forced a distinction between endangered and normal childhood. As with dangerousness, the need to deal with abnormality has produced modern narratives of expertise detailing the "normal" — though children are rarely referred to in these terms. Normality is the implicit standard against which abnormality is staked out and administered. Child abuse, more than any other issue in the twentieth century, has created an explosion of meaning around childhood. Many notions of childhood have come into play in health, legislative, and social policy arenas. And as child abuse became a key concern in many countries, so childhood, as the "most intensively governed sector of personal existence" (Rose 1989:121), took on new meanings. Childhood, then, is constituted as a social category at least partly through the rapid emergence of concern to identify and manage child abuse.

Childhood in Social Theory

A concern with meaning (hermeneutics) takes us to the places where meanings are created. A diversity of narrative and grand narrative enterprises converge on childhood, making it a significant nodal point in generating social theory. Childhood, however, has not had its central position in social theory acknowledged. Even where it appears to be a central analytic focus, childhood is often only a point of access to some broader social issue or agenda. This is also true of its status in this book, where childhood is part of an attempt to understand how the family is generated in the processes of administering it.

Even Aries' (1962) central work of reference on childhood is really an attempt to document the rise of the modern family in French imagery, thought, and social configurations. His thesis indicates the centrality of childhood in generating the family. Childhood, for some social theorists, is conceptualized as a strategic device in the management of populations. Foucault's *History of Sexuality* (1980), for example, sees children as the focus of moral, legal, medical, and social welfare interventions which bring about the regulation of family life. The mechanisms of this regulation are part of Foucault's (1980:77-131) most direct statement on power as a diffuse set of loosely regulatory operations. These regulatory operations are effected through the administrative actions of what Althusser (1972) refers to as the "ideological state apparatus" and which operates effectively around children through the education system, among other things. Donzelot (1979) explicitly locates children as a focus for the intervention of public agencies concerned with standards of care and education. These public agencies consequently regulate family life. But the regulation of family life, for Donzelot and for Foucault, is ultimately part of a bigger social project. This is the "disciplining" of populations which is seen as the key to success in competition between nations for economic development, trade, and expansion. Bell (1993), in the Foucauldian tradition, also suggests that childhood is a strategy: she suggests that our central concern should be to determine how childhood is deployed. Childhood may well be a strategy, but it is undoubtedly more than this. It is, as Bell (1993:393) also suggests, composed of a series of ambiguous and contested meanings. Childhood, Bell points out, is always being formulated and reformulated in legal and policy arenas. Unfortunately, she does not explore what these ambiguous and contested formulations and reformulations might be.

To maintain that childhood is only part of a broader social strategy is to maintain its analytical marginality in social theory. Childhood is an object of social analysis in its own right; its field of social meanings is worthy of investigation. Casting childhood simply as a strategy for social regulation is to neglect the project of unpacking its meanings in favour of documenting its effects on society as a whole. Of course, childhood has some important implications both for shaping the family and for organizing society as a whole, and I am not intending to deny its broader social significance. I merely suggest that some of its broader social implications are connected with its various meanings.

Most traditional sociological (as opposed to historical and philosophical) analyses of childhood conceptualize it as a family role, or as an age stage preceding adolescence and adulthood:

> The family is the central focus in the organization of the life course in all societies.... In childhood young people are most often defined, both in the minds of others and in their own minds, as children of their parents. This circumstance fits with the children's social and emotional dependence on their families ... the beginning of adolescence ushers in that phase in the life course when young people are encouraged to achieve an identity as autonomous individuals....(Fasick 1989:111)

Childhood in this analysis is a temporary stage in the life cycle. Its major purpose is to be a space in which the social reproduction of existing (adult) social relations and practices are secured.[1] Childhood in sociology serves as a short-hand explanation for the perpetuation of social forms. Having little social significance on its own, it is the adult world in preparation. James and Proutt (1990:7-8) point out that the study of childhood in the social sciences has been marked not by a lack of interest in children, but by their silence. The voices of children are primarily articulated by adults on behalf of children or as recovered memories of a past childhood. Childhood has featured as an age stage, as a strategy for social regulation, and as a place where adult learning takes place; but not as an object of social analysis in its own right.

Margaret and Michael Rustin's (1987:4-5) charting of the proliferation of childhood as a "social and emotional space (and as a distinctive) life stage in the latter half of the 19th century for a small privileged minority of the population, and increasingly, in this century for nearly all" avoids many of the pitfalls of sociological accounts. Conceptualizing childhood within psychoanalytic, sociological, and literary enterprise, and exploring the "imaginative and emotional aspects of children's experience," the Rustins examine the inner lives of children through their fantasies — a dimension which is sadly lacking in conventional sociological enterprise. Their work also conceptualizes childhood as an object of analysis in its own right (1987:3). They do, however, see childhood as having an ontological "reality" which can be described, rather than seeing it as a domain of shifting contextual meanings.

The grand narratives of psychoanalysis and developmental psychology are much more directly concerned than sociology or social theory with childhood as a central object of intellectual enterprise. These narratives provide important intellectual frameworks for those who are involved professionally with childhood. Although neither is solely the product of a concern with child abuse, both narratives have been strongly influenced by the demand to provide expertise on children, which has accompanied the emergence of child abuse as a target for social change.

One of the most significant narrative enterprises focused on childhood and affecting the ways in which we think about children is psychoanalysis. The proliferation of psychoanalysis in popular thought and imagery accords childhood a centrality in the explanation of adult self-identity or personhood. Childhood has, in popular culture, come to be seen as the place where the adult self is created. Indeed, it is difficult to imagine a conception of personhood which does not invoke some kind of account of childhood by way of explanation. How many times have we heard people explain their own character in this way: "Oh I was over disciplined/over indulged/never listened to/smacked/allowed to do what I wanted ... as a child'? The way we are is seen as being connected with the ways in which our childhoods were managed. Most people believe that their basic character and behaviour patterns were "shaped," but not necessarily determined, in childhood and we owe this insight to psychoanalysis. This hegemonic view of childhood has some very important implications in terms of child abuse. Defective childhoods produce defective adult personalities and a link between child abuse and mental health is thus sustained.

Alice Miller's (1987) controversial psychoanalytic perspective is one of the more popularly accessible contemporary accounts of childhood,[2] in part because it is so clearly and persuasively written. Her account of the history of social attitudes toward children from the eighteenth century on, which she views with the horror provided by contemporary psychoanalytic insight, concedes nothing to sociological analysis or to the practicalities of child rearing and contemporary family life:

> The former practice of physically maiming, exploiting and abusing children seems to have been gradually replaced in modern times by a form of mental cruelty that is masked by the scientific term child rearing....
>
> An enormous amount can be done to a child in the first two years: he or she can be moulded, dominated, taught good habits, scolded, and punished — without any repercussions for the person raising the child and without the child taking revenge. The

child will overcome the serious consequences of the injustices he
has suffered only if he succeeds in defending himself, ie., if he is
allowed to express his pain and anger. If he is prevented from
reacting in his own way because the parents cannot tolerate his
reactions (crying, sadness, rage) and forbid them by means of
looks or other pedagogical methods, then the child will learn to
be silent. The silence is a sign of the effectiveness of the pedagogical principles applied, but at the same time it is a danger signal
pointing to future pathological development.... I shall try to
demonstrate that neuroses are not the only tragic consequence of
repression.(Miller 1987:4)

Children emerge from this narrative as the victims of a parental and
pedagogical "violence" embedded in what passes for normal child-rearing practice. If "normal" child-rearing practices are abusive,what kind
of damage is then inflicted by behaviour that other psychoanalysts consider abusive?

While the strength of Miller's (1987:279) analysis lies in her discussion of the hidden power relationships embedded in the parent-child
relationship, her insight into power dynamics in the family leads her to
conclude that all forms of parenting are inherently pathological:
"Child rearing is basically directed not towards the child's welfare but
towards satisfying the parent's need for power and revenge" (Miller
1987:243).

The revenge to which Miller refers springs from the unfulfilled childhood needs of the parenting adult. This is a distinctively psychoanalytic construction of personhood, focusing on the minutiae of family
dynamics. Its sensitivity to the needs of children is so finely tuned that
parents should be immobilized by the fear that any action on their part
will seriously damage their children.

Psychoanalysis has justly laid claim to the expertise to explain child
abuse and offer therapeutic services to those who have been abused. As
far as child abuse is concerned two significant formulations emerge
from Miller's (1987:240) work which align it more closely with other
psychoanalytic (grand) narratives. The first is the relationship between
abuse and poor adult mental health already referred to. The second is

the victim/perpetrator relationship in which perpetrators are seen as historically having themselves been victims of abuse. Abuse, then, reproduces itself inter-generationally. These two propositions have secured a dominant place in narratives on child abuse because they assert the social significance of child abuse — abuse produces damaged people and social problems — and because they explain why child abuse occurs: people abuse because they were abused themselves. These are issues which are taken up in the chapters which follow on motherhood and fatherhood.

Reconstructions of childhood by the adult self have become a particularly contentious enterprise in cases of "recovered memories" of childhood sexual abuse. The legal and emotional battles that have ensued between adult "survivors" of sexual abuse and their "perpetrators" have been the object of legal battles involving damage suits in the United States. These battles hinge on a debate within psychoanalysis about the nature of childhood memory. Some therapists working with adult survivors see childhood as a crucial site of repressed and recoverable memories. They help clients recover their memories of abuse so that they can begin the healing process. Those accused of sexual abuse (and their supporters) contend that these memories are constructed rather than reconstructed in the therapeutic process under the guidance of therapists. The narrative containing the memory of abuse is seen as being worked up in collaboration between the analyst and the analysand. These false memories are organized in "the vague border region between what one is told about one's past and what one remembers for sure about it" (Kenny 1994:1).

These memories, it is argued, are amenable to "myth" because they reconstruct a childhood which is beyond conscious memory. Child abuse has pointed to the contestability of childhood as a field of memories. But childhood is not a field of memories dominated by children, but by adults reliving their childhoods. The voices of children, in fact, are rarely heard unmediated by adults.

A further set of narratives on childhood produced in developmental psychology makes childhood a specific kind of analytic space. The work of John Bowlby (cited in Riley 1983), and later, Michael Rutter (1984), among many others, has contributed significantly to understanding childhood in a particular way. Developmental psychology has had an impact on popular thought about children through the vast "practical advice to mothers" industry. This industry and its manuals dispense advice on how to take care of young children especially, explaining developmental stages and ways of dealing with behaviour difficulties. Nicholas Rose (1989) suggests that the construction of childhood through developmental psychology provides both a framework for understanding "normality" in childhood and a barrage of tests with which to measure it. Measuring normality in developmental terms allows the "troubled" and the "maladjusted" to be tracked (Rose 1989:121). The trajectories of normal development invoke two highly significant and related concepts: "child needs" and "emotional health."

While emotional health results from the meeting of child needs by effective parenting, child needs are in part a cultural construction. Different societies have different ideas about what children need, but child needs are organized in more "scientific" terms by developmental psychology (Woodhead 1990:63-73),which bases its conclusions on infant observations and experiments. This way of understanding childhood makes many demands upon parenting in the cause of child welfare. It also opens up the mother-child relationship to public scrutiny (Rose 1989:164). In constructing the image of the "normal" child, childhood comes complete with a set of instructions to parents on how to meet child needs and so guarantee emotional health. It is through psychology, Rose (1989:131) argues, that childhood becomes "an object of government through expertise" (Rose 1989:131). And child behaviour becomes the clue to the "emotional economy of the family" (Rose 1989:155). A "difficult" or "maladjusted" child is the sign that all is not well within the family. Operating in a Foucauldian framework, Rose suggests that childhood is a focus for social management strategies affecting the regulation of subjectivity and the interior of family life.

Rose is suggesting that families regulate their lives so as to broadly comply with expert narratives on children.

But we don't really know if this is the case. We don't know — because it is difficult to investigate — whether the "expert advice industry" affects the ways in which parents actually deal with their children. Parent-child interactions are private matters not easily open to scrutiny except on certain occasions. But developmental psychology *can* be seen to affect the performance of parenting in public. For example, it is now quite rare to see parents smack their children in public places, and anyone doing so would certainly attract attention and disapproval. In a Toronto shopping mall, I once drew a small crowd of spectators who gathered around to see how I would deal with my two-year-old who was throwing a tantrum. I became acutely aware that I was giving a public performance of motherhood which required a certain approach to childhood. In private I may well have been less patient and soothing and more exasperated.

The insights of development psychology are influential in decisions about whether or not there is a need to be concerned about protecting a child. Professional interventions around child abuse often see the state of the child as the key to the emotional economy of the family, as Rose suggests. A withdrawn child or a child who is not growing as s/he should, or a child who is not intellectually developing as s/he should, raises professional concerns. The measuring and charting of normality and abnormality is a hazardous business which renders childhood in particular terms. Childhood becomes a series of growth and developmental expectations: it is administratively invented in a particular way and in terms which are quite different from the childhood of psychoanalysis or the childhood of sociology. But without these measures of normality against which the troubled and the maladjusted can be "discovered," the detection of child abuse would be even more difficult than it is. Developmental psychology, like other professional narratives, is a series of techniques for speaking about childhood.

What follows is an attempt to understand some of the professional actions shaping the way we see the family through the administration of childhood by experts in the field. As I pointed out in the introduction, I am not studying these administrative actions directly, but rather I am looking at the *representation of these actions in narrative*. Actions are registered and discussed in narrative; and narratives of child expertise play a part in informing the practices making up child protection. But narrative and action are not the same thing: Action is about what child experts and professionals actually "do," whereas narrative is about the ways in which professionals represent those actions in the form of statements, writing, and reports of research. As soon as we reflect upon our actions we convert them into narrative. Even if I directly studied the actions of child protection workers, psychologists, psychiatrists, physicians, or lawyers working with abused children (which raises all sorts of ethical concerns), I would be in the business of converting these actions into narratives by writing about them. Instead, I use professionals' own narratives reflecting on what it is they do and why they do it. These professional narratives are intended as guides to practice and in the context of this book substitute for practice, although they are clearly not the same thing. Narratives, then, are not just theories or empty words; they organize and sustain concrete actions and forms of professional practice. They have definite social consequences.

The psychological and psychoanalytic narratives reviewed above provide authoritative sources of reference for a number of different professionals working with child abuse. Some of these narratives are more theoretical, but some are drawn from the healing work which both psychologists and psychoanalysts do with abused children. Psychological and psychoanalytic narratives are also influential in shaping popular thought about children and child-rearing practices. For these reasons it is important to understand the intellectual frameworks through which they invite us to "see" children. That such narrative conceptions of childhood also inform a multiplicity of pedagogical, legal, and social welfare interventions around childhood as a defensible, definable space in the social economy, is the point of the following pages. Practitioners who deal professionally with childhood draw upon as well as reformulate, through the administrative requirements of their own professions, the narratives of psychoanalysis and developmental psychology.[3] What Foucault (1980) and Donzelot (1979) refer to as the social management of childhood is organized through the practices of social workers, health workers, teachers, and guidance counsellors. Somewhere between practice and narrative the interventions of all concerned with child abuse issues have important consequences in reconfiguring the social meanings of the family. It is with these that the remainder of the chapter is concerned: with the multiple contested meanings of childhood in practice-oriented narratives around interventions to manage potentially abusing families, and with the ways in which childhood is seen in rendering it an object of administrative action.

Childhood as an object of legal protection

Some of the most significant social arenas in which childhood acquires a range of contested meanings and an administrative apparatus are legal. These arenas include the judiciary, the legislatures which make laws concerning children, and the ministries running child protection services which have a statutory basis. Childhood is, in practical terms, an object of legal protection. Children have certain minimum legal rights which can be pursued through legal channels. Those who violate childhood open themselves to criminal prosecution. This has always been so in modern times, but the manner in which childhood operates as a set of legally enforceable rights regularly changes. What follows is an attempt to sketch in some of the parameters of childhood in legislative terms as it applies in Canada, and in international convention.

Law is centrally important in the technical demarcation of childhood as a specific form of personhood from adulthood. In most Canadian provinces the boundary between childhood and adulthood is between sixteen and eighteen, and is set out in the legal codes which govern child sexuality and child protection. In Québec, for example, the rights which come with childhood are specified in the Québec

Charter of Human Rights and Freedoms and in the Civil Code. This sets out the basic framework of child rights within which the Youth Protection Act offers more specific guidelines (Federal-Provincial Working Group 1994:69).

The boundary between childhood and adulthood is an uneven and moving boundary. Of course, it is under constant review as social conditions and practices change. But the boundary between childhood and adulthood is also differently positioned around sexuality, alcohol consumption, marriage, driving licences, and the exercise of citizenship through voting rights. All of these rights come into play at different ages, so that childhood is gradually surrendered with the acquisition of adult rights. The most contentious point of this boundary concerns sexual activity. There is, in many countries and states, an on-going debate about whether or not sexual activity is legitimately a child or an adult domain. In the Netherlands, for example, both heterosexual and homosexual activity has been legalized for twelve-year-olds, so that charges of under-aged sex are not laid unless there is a complaint. This is presented as a codification of what already happens in practice (*Independent on Sunday,* 18 Nov. 1990). In this context sexual activity is a qualified feature of childhood. This is not the case in Canada, Britain or in most states in the United States, where legal sexual activity is attached to one of the lower limits of the boundaries of adulthood. The boundary between childhood and adulthood is best conceptualized as a buffer zone of rights to participation in different kinds of activities. The other boundary of childhood — its beginning — is organised around conception, the gestational age of foetuses and birth. This boundary is organized by moral, scientific/medical, and religious debates about abortion.

Childhood became an object of international legal protection when it was taken up by the League of Nations in 1924, although both "childhood" and "rights" had a different range of meanings at that time. Current international recognition that childhood is a particular form of personhood is organized around a notion of "human rights" and set out in the United Nations Declaration on the Rights of the Child. Following the lead of the United Nations, the Government of Quebec's (1993:9) Commission de Protection de Droits de la Jeunesse conceptualizes "les enfants" as "les plus vulnerables de notre société," asserting firmly that children are "sujets de droit." Any statement of legally construed rights necessarily stipulates what those rights consist of. Childhood was conceptualized in the United Nations declaration as a protected space: "childhood is entitled to special care and assistance," bringing with it the right to "identity, including nationality, name and family relations...," the right of children to form and express their own views, and "freedom of thought, conscience and religion" (1989 "Convention on the Rights of the Child" cited in the Report of the Special Advisor to the Ministry of National Health and Welfare on Child Sexual Abuse in Canada 1991:3-8). Internationally, the rights of children are extensive and mirror those of adults — human rights — in international convention. But the enforceability of such rights is another matter. The rights set out in the United Nations Convention are presented as the cornerstone of federal child policy in the Canadian government report on child abuse cited above (1991:11). In that report child rights secure a protected space from violence and sexual exploitation. This is significantly extended in Quebec by section 39 of the Quebec Charter of Human Rights and Freedoms which states that "all children are entitled to the protection, security and attention of their parents..." (Federal-Provincial Working Group 1994:72).

Despite this seemingly extensive recognition of childhood as the site of human and social rights, legal practice has been slow to accommodate children. Adjusting the rules of evidence in court proceedings, for example, to take account of the different ways in which children "tell stories" in sexual abuse cases is still in the review stages, as Bill C-15 shows. Relaxing the rules of evidence, as Bill C-15 did, would make it easier to secure conviction in abuse cases, although it is not clear how increasing conviction rates is actually a solution to the problem of child abuse within the family. Also under review in Bill C-15 are experiments establishing the veracity of play as storytelling, as well as the issue of videoing and screens in courts so that children do not have to face their accused attacker.

In practice, legally construed child human rights are only effective when they are enforceable. This is especially true in families where agency surveillance operates because there is suspicion that children are being harmed. Here child advocacy by social welfare workers can be effective in securing a stronger and more highly defended negotiating position for children against their abusers. The enforcement of rights, but not the mere existence of rights alone, can secure some measure of child empowerment. The courts and the powers they give to front-line child protection workers are hence highly significant. These powers can force parents to moderate and account for their behaviour. They can restrain parents and remove children from the family home.

Social welfare narratives

Social welfare narratives concerned with childhood comprise a genre rather than a single perspective. They are connected with two dimensions of collective wellbeing: the family and the society as a whole. A range of meanings attach themselves to childhood in these narratives, and we will briefly consider some of them.

Childhood is frequently conceptualized as indissoluble from family life, embedded within the collective welfare of the family as though it had no separate, much less conflicting, constituencies and interests. In a way this is a reasonable position. Families have to negotiate a way of balancing the interests and well-being of their members when these operate in a collective living space. But this view of childhood buries it within the requirements and interests of the family as a whole. In practice, the interests of the family are dominated by adults. This, of course, contests the view that children must be seen in terms of their own "best interests" and that these interests are an object of special legal protection. This view is the rationale of social welfare casework, which is concerned with child protection. In practice, social workers have to cut a path between the competing interests of family members, which are often bound up with some complex, ambivalent, and contradictory feelings. Take, for example, this statement by a caseworker about the complexity of family interests involved in a physical abuse case:

> I received a physical abuse complaint a few months ago. The initial complaint was of an eight year old boy receiving strappings. I interviewed the little boy at school and he disclosed the strappings. I went to the family home, concerned about what response my presence would elicit. Mom was very upset at first, frustrated at the system. She had told someone herself about the strappings and had been asking for help. The result she saw was a social worker at her door....She talked about not liking her son and how bad that made her feel. We talked about isolation, feeling guilt over the choices your kids make, frustration for a system that can appear hostile to clients. She had prepared herself for me to apprehend her son. But because of this woman's openness and genuine caring, we were able to set up some solid survival plans that would decrease the household stress, ensure her son's protection, and address some of his mental health issues. (Callahan 1993:70)

Although child protection workers operate within some of the general parameters and professional practices evident in social welfare narratives, there is, in practice, considerable flexibility and intuitiveness surrounding the ways in which they do their work.

Childhood in social welfare narratives is also conceptualized as an opportunity for the reconstruction of "dysfunctional" families. This narrative rendering of childhood links two dimensions of collective welfare: the family and the broader society. This link comes from developmental psychology and psychoanalysis. It is usually a bid for damage limitation and corresponds with some well-intentioned claims upon social resources. The general argument is that children are an "investment" in the future of society as a whole, and it is this which makes them worthy recipients of public expenditure:

> Policies concerning children and families are priorities on both Canadian and U.S. agendas today because of widespread alarm

about the future of vulnerable children. Businesses worry about the shrinking pool of youngsters with the skills to operate in today's high-tech economy — the president of Xerox says that the "work force is running out of qualified people." There is a growing awareness that early disadvantage and inadequate health, mental health, education and social services are linked to a lack of skills among young adults on whom we must depend to do tomorrow's work and keep our nations prosperous. (Schorr 1991:437)

This extract is taken from a paper published in the *Canadian Journal of Psychiatry* and is arguing for breaking the cycle of disadvantage with broadly based community initiatives in place of individual treatment. Childhood thus presents opportunities to challenge the reproduction of family dysfunction and its negative social and economic implications. Children are hence seen as an important social agency in securing social change in the direction of individual and collective prosperity.

In practice, these noble sentiments demanding social justice in the cause of collective interest often come down to an attempt to identify and reconstruct the "problem" families of an "underclass" of welfare recipients by focusing on their offspring. This underclass is usually narratively constructed so as to comprise an undifferentiated range of social problems: child abuse, teen pregnancy, arrests for violent crime, and long-term dependency on welfare (Hechtman 1989:569; Schorr 1991:437-439), and it is offered as a target for social reform. It is by no means clear that distinctive social problems cluster together in this manner, but that they are seen to do so is in itself significant. Certainly the poor are overrepresented in welfare interventions around children (Martin 1985:55). Childhood is interpreted as the place where the cycle of deprivation can be arrested, presenting the possibility of broad social reform. Childhood, then, is certainly accorded an autonomy, a sense of agency, and a social significance which goes beyond the family. Childhood is collective property: it is the place where a sense of social citizenship is forged.

Childhood is also seen as an important social resource in the broader social, commercial, and economic viability of the nation (Schorr

1991:437). This is especially so in the context of recent demographic changes shifting the age structure of the population toward the upper end of the scale (Report of the Special Advisor to the Minister of National Health and Welfare on Child Sexual Abuse in Canada 1991:11). In this context national prosperity becomes the responsibility of a shrinking number of younger people whose efforts are supporting a large number of elderly. The defence of childhood hence becomes more than a humanitarian concern; it is a precious resource, at least in the "developed" countries,[4] where its defence has become a matter of social efficiency. The need to reduce, and eventually eliminate, child abuse as a waste of precious resources thus becomes a highly politicized national project.

Childhood, then, occupies a number of positions of significance in the social welfare genre of narratives. Childhood is a form of agency for the reform of what is seen as an underclass: it is an inseparable part of the definition and accomplishments of a family unit; it has become a means of expressing a form of social citizenship; and it is an important social and economic resource in securing national prosperity. Childhood is about the better management of the world of adults. When childhood becomes something to be managed and administered by front-line agencies armed with professional expertise, it also becomes much more.

Endangered Childhood

In some of the narratives concerned with therapeutic intervention around child abuse, endangerment and vulnerability are major themes. The endangered child is seen as the target, object, and product of a certain kind of (dangerous) parenting. These are issues to which I will return. This construction of childhood as endangered establishes it as a "type" and displaying a constellation of behavioural characteristics. The Parent and Child Therapy Society, for example, identifies the endangered child in the following terms:

Abused children often lack the spontaneous desire to play cre-
atively — their play is often repetitious, indicating a desire to be
neat and tidy, rather than a wish to explore the material or the
world around them. It is often said that abused children lack basic
play skills — they do not seem to know how to jump, run, handle
paints, modelling clay. Further more they often do not know that
to play is their right, since they sometimes ask permission of the
adult to play. The lack of joy in life, which is often a noticeable
characteristic of severely abused children, is sometimes very obvious in the mechanical way in which they use toys and equipment.
The usual curiosity to explore, which is the natural heritage of
most children, seems to be severely diminished in certain abused
children.

Abused children usually relate poorly to both adults and other
children.... Abused children are often extremely angry children
who have a belligerent defiant attitude to peers and adults. Less
frequently they can be excessively pleasing compliant children.
(Parent and Child Therapy Society 1984:59)

Specifically in cases of suspected sexual abuse, behaviour indicating
endangeredness includes signs of trauma, sometimes diagnosed as
"traumatic stress disorder," anxiety, loss of memory, and loss of self-
esteem (Bentovim 1988:26). The "Cinderella syndrome" child who
wears ill-fitting clothes and the child exhibiting "inappropriate" behaviour (Bentovim 1988:27-9) alert professionals to the possibility of
endangerment. "Unnatural" levels of social aggression, or sexual
behaviour, and a deficit of "normal" social competence operate as the
signs of an underlying problem of endangerment and a certain kind of
vulnerability (Sawula 1989). The endangered child in these comments
is a collection of psycho-social abnormalities played out in behavioural terms. In this acting out, the child is seen to be telling a story about
the private conduct of family life: a story which can be interpreted by
child experts.

Implicit in the detailing of endangerment are notions of normality
and naturalness which are never openly specified nor subjected to crit-

ical analysis, but which nonetheless serve as a standard against which abnormality is discovered in much the way Rose (1989) suggests. The normal child, at least by implication, does not display inappropriate behaviour, anger, poor playing skills or poor social relationships. But the normal child is not the target of intervention and so does not need to be rendered in more precise, administrative terms.

Childhood as indicator

Implicit in the meaning of childhood as endangered is the notion that children operate as the conscious or unwitting "indicators" of family dynamics. Child behaviour tells a story about the family which can be interpreted by the trained observer: the child is the crucial point of access to private family conduct. The child's behaviour is important evidence in the detection and prediction of abuse. Childhood in this context is an index of the ways in which adults privately respond to children. For example, children who show signs of endangerment, who run away, who turn to prostitution or to excessive substance and alcohol use are in fact often thought to be indirectly "reporting" abuse (McGregor and Dutton 1988:3-8). Certain forms of childhood signal risk and raise suspicion among child experts that all is not well in the family.

Risk is a key concept in child abuse narratives. It is given a potency by the urgency it conveys, by the centrality of its appearance in narrative, and by the lack of precision and critical enquiry which surrounds its use. There is a large literature concerned with risk and risk assessment as these are centrally important issues for front-line caseworkers. Brender, Gagnon & Dubrow's *Child Sexual Abuse: Risk factors For Negative Long-Term Effects* (undated), a report published by the Family Violence Prevention Division of Health and Welfare Canada, for example, lists the voluminous literature dealing with risk assessment. The stakes around risk prediction are high, as Callahan notes in the context of child protection:

> There are few other jobs with a mandate to enter the privacy of family life, make judgements about the behaviour of family

members, and take actions that can alter significantly the membership and functioning of that family.... If mistakes are made,
children may die, parents may break down, and families may be
permanently damaged. (Callahan 1993:73)

Risk has different meanings in different agency practices. Front-line
child protection workers are often called upon to make fast decisions in
dramatic situations (Callahan 1993:74); some child protection workers
report developing a sense of risk through experience.

> I was working with a thirteen year old girl who had been a per-
> manent ward but who had recently returned home to live with her
> mother. She was originally taken into care because she had been
> badly burned in a house fire set by her mother's angry common-
> law spouse. As a result she had quite disfiguring scars on her face,
> chest and abdomen.
>
> The mother called me to her home and announced that the
> child was pregnant, and wanted help in getting an abortion for
> her. Both the child and mother told me that she had intercourse
> with a classmate at school, and the child told me she did not want
> to give me the boy's name. I knew intuitively that this was not true
> and interviewed the child alone the next day. She disclosed that
> her uncle had raped her and had, in fact, sexually molested sever-
> al of her female cousins. (Callahan 1993:71)

Physicians also work with risk indicators. In their case these are about
bodily signs and the stories of parents explaining those signs.

Risk is frequently deployed with a range of other concepts which are
equally poorly specified but which refer to styles and standards of
parental child care. Risk can mean anything from "poor," "substandard" or "ineffective" parenting to lethal, ongoing physical and sexual
violation. While there may be some agreement in practice about what
constitutes serious physical and sexual violation, the concepts "poor,"
"substandard," and "ineffective" are open to wide interpretation.
Many social critics of the lifestyles of the poor have ridden the band-
wagon of child abuse by linking sloppy or substandard parenting with

risk. Being "at risk" has become a rationale for researching certain (usually poor) populations, and often the precise nature of the "risk" in question becomes disconnected from its social consequences, and the lives of the poor are scavenged for yet more signs of social failure. As a member of a university Ethics Committee reviewing research protocols, I was asked to consider a research proposal submitted by a psychologist who wanted to continue with a longitudinal study of an "at risk population" he had identified many years earlier. When I asked the representatives from his department, because it was not clear from the description of the research, what this population was at risk of, it transpired that no one could remember. Perhaps they were most at risk of being over-researched by psychologists. At risk has become a general description, the most significant part of which is poverty.

The ambiguity surrounding risk has not hindered its entry into medical narratives, where it achieves a "scientific" rigour in acquiring an "epidemiology."[5] The Montreal Children's Hospital, for example, conducted a study which it published as the "Epidemiology of Risk Factors in Family Violence" (1988). This study contains no discussion of what risk might consist of — assuming a broad professional consensus which did not need to be discussed — but goes on to plot its distribution. Around the distribution of risk emerge two populations of "high" and "low" risk families. Similarly, but in psychological terms, McGregor and Dutton (1988:9) compare rates of sexual abuse among "problem" and "normal" populations as though these were discrete groups with identifiable social characteristics. The epidemiology of risk ultimately relies on social categorizations. Individuals identified in psychological and medical terms are linked with social categories: the unemployed, the young, substance abusers, and so on. These social categories then become charged with the individual psychological difficulties with which they are associated. What is intended as a means of prediction becomes a stigmatizing and short-hand way of indicating a range of undesirable behaviours and lifestyles. As far as childhood is concerned, the social distribution of risk has some important implications in designating 'types' of childhood in medical and psychological narratives.

Risk also has a currency in the narratives generated around perinatal medicine. Medical intervention around childbirth is seen as a win-

dow of opportunity onto family relationships at a crucial point at [103]
which the family is being generated or extended. The infant is thought
to act as a catalyst in generating family dynamics which are "played
out" under the medical gaze. These dynamics are thought to contain
vital clues about the level of risk inside the family. The perinatal period is hence seen as a vantage point from which to make early predic-
tions of risk, and to offer interventions in the family. Perinatal medicine
has acquired this position due to the emphasis placed on "prevention,"
a highly problematic concept in the context of child abuse. This window onto the family is primarily aimed at the mother and so will be
discussed in the next chapter, but it also produces a description of
childhood as a list of risk factors.

The "high-risk" infant demonstrates signs of an underlying problem
from birth. Low birth weight is the medical index of risk and is often
used to substitute for a range of social pathologies, and to provide a
rationale for medical intervention:

> Among infants low birth weight is a potential predictor of risk.
> Low birth weight can be the result of premature delivery or inad-
> equate prenatal care by the mother. In either case the child requires
> special care and attention. The Maternal Child Health Branch of
> Manitoba Health considers 2500 grams to be a normal birth
> weight. Newborns weighing less are cause for concern.... Any
> child who is not thriving (according to weight) should be evaluat-
> ed for neglect.... (External Review into Matters Relating to the
> System of Dealing with Child Abuse in Winnipeg 1987:305-6)

Ledger and Williams' (1981) work, based in British Columbia and
drawing upon the findings of similar work done in the United States, is
highly influential in directing practice in Canadian perinatal medicine.
This is seen in the extent to which their risk indicators are reproduced
to guide the practices of health workers throughout the country. The
high risk (endangered) infant is typically "premature," "physically and
mentally defective," a "difficult feeder," "unresponsive," or "irritable
and difficult to console." The "defective" child may also be perceived
by his or her mother in the postpartum and prenatal period as

deformed or monstrous (Ledger and Williams 1981:117). Such observations clearly rely heavily upon the medical staff's construction of the meaning of the mother-infant interaction they observe. These issues are taken up in the chapter on motherhood below.

Controlling indicators

Risk to children is also a bargaining point between mothers and child protection agencies. It is not simply the case that agencies impose notions of risk, but mothers also use a narrative of risk in order to gain resources for her family or affect the outcome of agency intervention. The extract which follows is taken from a report written by a social worker who effectively complies with the demands of a mother who wants her adolescent son placed in temporary foster care. The narrative contained in the file (the source of which cannot, for reasons of confidentiality, be divulged) constructed by the social worker leans towards the conclusion of the mother.

> Ms X. stated that she attended a parent effectiveness group and that she found that interesting but Y's [son's] behaviour continued to be problematic. However, Ms X. did not beat Y ... though over time her frustration and patience were "taxed" and about two months ago she started beating Y again.... At the present time Ms X. is incapable of managing Y's behaviour. Ms X would rather have her son at home with her than on placement, but feels that she can no longer manage his difficult behaviour and is concerned that she will hurt her child, because of her inappropriate responses [beating him with a belt].

In cases where people have few resources, any kind of respite from parenting is welcomed. Clients also learn to manipulate the narratives of child protection so as to secure outcomes which suit them. This mother is clearly playing the "risk game" with her social worker by suggesting that she cannot be relied upon not to beat her son. In this way she is exercising her own forms of power in which she positions herself within the terms of the narrative of risk.

The following story is that of an adolescent street child and drug user. It reflects on the circumstances in which she disclosed her mother's physical abuse to a teacher and also shows how those who are the object of risk assessment are able to control information.

Child: "I can't take this money," I protested.
Teacher: "Why not?"
C: "Because if my mother finds it she'll take it off me and buy something."
T: "What will she buy?" Miss MacDonald prodded. "Some beer maybe?"
C: "Maybe," I answered. She wasn't going to get me to say my mother was a lush and a beater. "And if she doesn't take the money off me she'll think I stole it," I added thinking I'd get the subject away from my mother's drinking.
T: "Why would she think you stole it? Do you steal things sometimes?" Miss MacDonald asked.
C: "No," I don't know why but I told her the truth. "Only when my mother is drunk and I steal fifty cents to buy some fish and chips for lunch."
T: "And what does she do to you when she finds out?" she probed gently.
C: "She has this plastic brush, and she makes me put my hands on the table so she can smash them," I confessed to the horrified teacher.
C: "That's nothing, she does lots worse. And then she calls me bad names and says she'll kill me if I tell anyone." (Sharon's story, Webber 1991:68)

A different kind of story of risk is told here by a native adolescent who grew up on a reserve and who learned intuitively to hide his family situation from the "authorities." This, too, is a kind of power through control.

That's not to say that I didn't understand my people's way of life on the reserve. I understood it alright: alcoholism. From my grandparents on down, all my relatives were alcoholic. Through my eyes, as a child, that seemed normal. I never felt different from the other children and families around me.

But I felt lonely and scared almost all the time. My parents would go out on drunks — for several days to a week at a time. We had no supervision at all. As the eldest of four children, and only a very young child myself, I was expected to take care of the little ones. I don't think anyone ever warned me about authorities, but I knew exactly what to do if a car pulled up with white people in it: hide my brothers and my sister, fast. My father was a skilled carpenter but there was hardly ever any work on the reserve. He moved us around to other reserves, looking for jobs, but it never got him anywhere. Instead of working, he drank and abused us: very severe, regular lickings with electrical cords. At the time I had no concept of abuse, though I hated the way he treated us and started running away when I was very young.... In spite of the way he abused us all, he was — somehow — my hero. (Ray's story, Webber 1991:228-9)

These graphic and harrowing stories based on insider experience of abuse have a dimension which official stories and narratives of childhood expertise cannot capture. They are stories which show that professionals do not have a monopoly over power in dealing with families over risk. Risk is bound up with some complex negotiations in which the objects of assessment manipulate risk, engage in selective disclosure, and collude in covering up aspects of their family life. The story of the native also raises questions about risk in a context where life is circumscribed by all manner of risks organized by poverty and alcoholism. His story questions the positioning of risk and normality in professional narratives.

Endangerment, Risk, and Poverty

It was noted in the last chapter that the risk of child abuse has a special relationship in narrative to poverty. The family and personal habits of the poor have, of course, been matters of public concern in Europe since the eighteenth century (Donzelot 1979) and in Canada since the nineteenth century (Valverde 1991, McLaren 1990). Poor children are still a major target for social management, a position which is re-enforced by the emergence of child abuse as a social concern. This concern with poverty has had an impact on the conceptualization of childhood: the "throwaway child" or the "unwanted child" is unquestioningly presented as the child of the poor family (Volpe 1989:3); modern disposable childhood is conceptualized as the potential target of parental violence, sexual abuse, and neglect. In the Cleveland child abuse cases in Britain in 1987, the more upscale social position of the families whose children were removed on the diagnosis of sexual abuse by controversial diagnostic methods (the anal dilation test), led at least one doctor not to see (because he did not believe) the sexual abuse discovered by his colleagues:

> I am absolutely satisfied in my own judgement that they were clearly families in which the question of buggery was quite inconceivable. (Held, cited in Campbell 1988:56)

Is there a *kind* of family in which the "question of buggery" *is* conceivable? Clearly in this doctor's mind there is.

The children of the poor are implicated in multiple forms of social pathology, such as drugs, crime, and prostitution, to which new emerging forms can and are always being added without disrupting the structure of the narrative. Although there is mounting evidence from researchers that the risk of child abuse is classless (Gelles and Strauss 1988, cited in Volpe 1989:4), "evidence" is immaterial. There is a well established (narrative) connection between poverty and a range of social problems, and this connection is difficult to disrupt. Some accounts of poverty are, however, more sympathetic:

> Parents told us that poverty means never having quite enough of anything and always being afraid that because of it, they'll lose their health, their home, or worst of all, their children. They spoke of their anguish when their children go into care, and of a different anguish when their children return to find that nothing

has changed at home. Parents stressed over and over again that they do not choose to live in poverty but that with high unemployment, low income assistance and a seemingly endless number of administrative barriers in their way, they could not escape. (Community Panel Family and Children's Services Legislation Review in British Columbia 1992)

Child abuse has become absorbed into the conceptual clustering of poverty and social pathology and is absorbed in a particular conceptualization of childhood as endangered.

Victimhood and Dangerousness

Implicit in some of the constructions of childhood considered in this chapter is a broader debate about guilt and innocence. Are children in any sense culpable for the abuse they suffer or are they its innocent victims? A review of professional analyses of child abuse shows that the dominant narrative theme is to construe children as victims, and childhood as a state of vulnerability. This interpretation of victimhood is implied by analyses which see childhood as jeopardized by adult behaviour and those which see childhood as an indicator of dysfunctional family dynamics. The caveat to this is found in the medical narratives which suggest that children with difficult behaviour (over which the children have, by implication, some control) may be in some ways culpable for their own victimhood. But then narratives on victimhood often move between sympathy and victim-blaming. This is especially evident in narratives on spousal abuse which hold women responsible, in part, for their victimization.

Chalin and Lewittes' (1988:2-3) review of clinical research studies (funded by the Family Violence Division of Health and Welfare Canada) refers to "clinical populations of victims" as though they were a "scientifically" demarcated category of the population. The victim population (like the at-risk population) is discussed in class, gendered, and racialized terms. In many of the narratives examined in writing this book, victimhood has a strong class dimension. It is the children of the poor who overwhelmingly make up the victim population because

their parents are more violent, less able to provide the material necessi-
ties for healthy lives, more stressed or simply more supervised by professionals looking for problems than others. This association between
victimhood and poverty is contested, however, by another major
(Canadian) source of commentary about children as victims: the federal and provincial government reports discussed in Chapter Two. In
these reports children are collapsed into more general categories of victims, which include women and native populations. Here, in place of
class, victimhood is racialized and gendered.

Racialization in this Canadian context focuses on native communities and sexual abuse. The authoritative Badgley Report (1984:17) pro-
poses a hierarchy of victims in which aboriginal peoples emerge as the
most victimized. This ethnicization of victimhood around sexual abuse
links abuse with a range of community pathologies which trace their
origins to the aggressive policies of assimilation of the Anglo/French
Canadian majority. Care should be taken with asserting a connection
between aboriginal peoples and abuse, since assimilationism is only
one of the more sympathetic explanations offered to account for abuse.
Other potential explanations (a greater predisposition to violence for
example) are far more pathologizing of aboriginal people.

The gendered nature of the victim population is especially clear in
the early research on sexual abuse by Finkelhor in the United States.
Finkelhor conceptualizes the sexually abused child as female. Even
some recent epidemiological studies claim that

> Analysis revealed that females comprised 75% to 100% of victims.
> In the National Hospital Survey, 86.3% of sexually assaulted vic-
> tims under the age of 16 were female. Eighty-seven percent to
> 100% of the assailants were male. (Chalin & Lewittes 1988:2-3)

This is certainly an overstatement of the gender dimensions of victimhood, as counter-evidence is provided by those who note the growing masculinization of victimhood (the British Columbia Task Force
on Family Violence 1992:136, for example). And the feminization of
the child victim is an especially dangerous tendency: not only does it
confirm broader social stereotypes of female passivity, it causes us to

overlook the extent to which male children are abused.

There are accounts of power and gender dynamics within the family which contest these professional narratives' conceptions of victimhood and its gendered dynamics. Shere Hite's (1994) stories of the (American) family's internal emotional dynamics and sexual scripts are not intended to explicitly discuss abuse in parent-child relationships, yet many of the first-person accounts she relates are about sexual tensions and physical violence between parents and children. One of her themes is the ways in which daughter-father relationships are organized by awareness of sexuality (Hite 1994:180-192). These are stories about power, influence and flirtation. Take this story of a young girl's feelings about her father:

> He used to wake me up from my naps in the most shy way — by patting me on the head just very softly, stroking my hair for a minute. I loved the feeling of his hands, the expression of tenderness on his face. As soon as I woke up he would stop — as though I shouldn't see his expression, as though this kind of touch between us was forbidden.

And this story of a boy's feelings about his father:

> During adolescence I had erotic fantasies of being caressed and approved of by my father. I was well into my twenties before I began to work on these feelings. What I realized was that I had very powerful urges for love and confirmation to flow between us...I haven't felt sexual desire for my mother because we are very close, and we know how much we love each other. (Hite 1994:253)

Another theme in Hite's narratives concerns the dynamics of power and violence within the family:

> I [reports a young woman] hated his [my father's] temper and domineering manners, I hated the way my mother served him all the time, and the way he considered us property all the time because we depended on him for support. (Hite 1994:198).

These comments place the issue of family violence and sexuality within a broader context than the discussions which are more directly concerned with recounting experiences of abuse. They make the point that
family behaviour may most effectively be seen as part of a continuum:
that sexuality is not a straightforward issue of victim and victimizer.
Hite's stories of the complexity surrounding sexuality contest the point
made by some of the professional narratives in the last chapter, which
divide families into the dangerous and the benign. They also contest
those professional narratives which assert the gendered nature of victimhood.

Hite's and the others' accounts of childhood related in this chapter
are not really child voices, but adult voices remembering childhood.
These adolescent and adult reconstructions of childhood contain the
consciousness that childhood abuse is a story which can be told along
with similar stories told by others. A context in which to tell these stories, which would otherwise remain untold, is consciously opened up
with the development of child abuse as a social issue. Adult victims are
"invited" to confess; the terms under which children themselves tell stories of abuse are quite different. A child telling the story to a therapist,
social worker or doctor (sometimes recorded in "disclosure" videos
which are horrifying to watch and which can later be used as evidence
to verify the story) also has a context. The child is being invited to tell
the story, but these stories are not really confessions in the same way as
adult stories are. Instead, they are naive re-enactments of events, a narrative told in actions and gestures. A child does not necessarily have the
kind of reflexiveness about abuse to see it as an "abnormality." It is this
reflexiveness which allows abuse to be positioned as a social issue in
narrative terms.

The victim status of childhood is most visibly challenged around the
boundaries of childhood and adulthood. It is around these boundaries
that victims move from innocence to culpability, and mark the transition to adulthood and the potential status of perpetrator. Victims of
family dysfunction may have all sorts of resources such as therapy
placed at their disposal before they reach the age of majority. After that
time they are routinely seen as "bad" and deserving of punishment
instead of treatment. The victim status of childhood is also challenged

in other narratives and agency networks. A brief review of popular and criminal justice narratives makes the point that constructions of childhood are tied in with particular clusters of narratives from particular agencies. Victim narratives are most closely tied to social welfare and therapeutic interventions with children. Quite another story is told in popular narratives and the narratives of the criminal justice system, which in certain circumstances conceptualize children not as endangered victims but as dangerous.

Dangerous children, who in many ways belong to the nineteenth century, are the counterpart of the child victim. This understanding of childhood makes fleeting appearances, inevitably around some heinous act committed by children. An example of the interpretation of children as dangerous emerged in Britain around the well-publicized murder of two-year-old James Bulger by two eleven-year-old boys. "Monster" and "evil" were two often repeated descriptions applied to the boys, both in the process of criminal prosecution, and in the popular uproar surrounding the case (Sereny, *Independent on Sunday*, 6 Feb. 1994). In excluding from the legal proceedings the issue of *why* the boys had murdered, the interpretation of them as victims of damaging parenting was ruled out. The remaining explanation was that they were just plain "evil." Indeed, this assessment was reflected in their sentencing to ten years of imprisonment. This sentence was later overturned by the intervention of the (Conservative) Home Secretary who, anxious to appease the "hang 'em and flog 'em" lobby, controversially raised their sentences to fifteen years.

A similar furore surrounded the brutal murder of an elderly Montreal priest and his wife in 1995 by three boys, the youngest of whom was thirteen. The differences in the treatment of (if not the public opinion about) these boys (the thirteen-year-old was tried as a child and got the maximum sentence of three years plus two years' supervision) from those involved in the Bulger murder point to some important differences between Britain and Canada in the area of child dangerousness, although the popular narratives of outrage sounded very much the same. The *Montreal Gazette* (8 April 1995) ran a story on "Children who Kill" which commented on the "savagery" and "brutality" of the boys and took the opportunity to review past murders by children: "Louis Morissette, a psychiatrist at the Pinel Institute in Montreal, [it was reported] agreed that adolescents are becoming dehumanised" (*Montreal Gazette* 8 April 1995:B8).

Psychological explanations may dominate the official view that something must have gone desperately wrong in their childhoods to produce such an act. Yet the fact that the two older boys were to be tried as adults (they ended up plea-bargaining), and the fact that the media are evaluating the danger factor posed by adolescent boys, are both highly significant in contextualizing childhood as dangerous.

Conclusions

This chapter has been concerned with mapping some of the multiple, ambiguous, and contested meanings attached to childhood in rendering it an object of professional administrative action. Childhood is variously conceptualized as an object of legal protection and special human rights. It is both a special, defensible space, and an inseparable dimension of family life. It is an opportunity for the reconstruction of problem families, and it is an important agency in effecting social reform. Childhood is also a resource and a key to collective national prosperity. It is a political project and an expression of social (as opposed to individual) citizenship. Childhood is also about endangerment and vulnerability. It is an indicator of family dynamics and family failure, and a catalyst in the playing-out of family relationships. Childhood both signifies, and offers the prospect of redemption of, the problematic world of adult relationships which are embedded in family life. Childhood is about risk, defectiveness and disposability. It is about victimhood and dangerousness.

Furthermore, childhood is a highly invested social construct. It has multiple meanings which are embedded in the practice-narratives in which it is invoked as an object of administrative action. It is also as marginal in professional narratives as it is in social analysis and in sociological narrative, where it also features as a means to an end rather than as a central object of intellectual and social enquiry. All of the meanings of childhood outlined in this chapter are really about accessing, understanding, sustaining, and reforming the world of adults.

Ultimately, even in the context of child abuse, childhood is a social mechanism of some sort, and this is significantly signalled in the absence of children's voices in the narratives.

Notes

1. Examples of this kind of writing include Frank Fasick (1989) 'Socialisation Beyond Childhood' in K. Ishwaran (ed) *Family and Marriage* Toronto: Wall and Thompson or Marlene Mackie 'Primary Socialisation in Cross Cultural Context' in G.N. Ramu (ed) *Marriage and the Family in Canada Today* Scarborough: Prentice Hall

2. This is not to deny the very significant contributions of some of the great psychoanalysts to this field, such as Winnicott, Melanie Klein, and Anna Freud.

3. Child protection and agencies managing child abuse do not simply replay grand narratives of childhood. They rather deploy them in various ways, organized by the practical and administrative requirements of their own professions and fields of expertise.

4. Childhood in poorer and developing countries where children are the explicit object of population control programmes is quite differently construed.

5. The epidemiology of child abuse was discussed in passing in Chapter Two.

ADMINISTERING MOTHERHOOD

THE social attention paid to expert commentaries on child "needs" has placed some heavy demands on mothers. Between this attention to the experts on children and the contemporary work of feminist scholars, motherhood has become a central object of social commentary. As the needs of children were asserted by experts, so feminist scholars took them on. But they did so in a rather limited way, focusing on theories of "maternal deprivation" (Riley 1983). Mother absence, according to the experts, was the source of all childhood pathology. Feminists did not generally challenge the concept of child needs; they did not examine the social construction of these needs or what they meant in terms of the minutiae of mothering activities. Child needs were taken as a "given," and feminists argued about who was responsible for meeting those needs. Feminists were more concerned that the social responsibility for child rearing be shared with fathers, with other family members, and with professional day-care services than with deconstructing the content of child needs. Feminists hence missed a political opportunity to re-think what childhood meant. Instead, they accepted it and tried to share it around. The reason they did this was that there was no space in which to have a debate about childhood. Discussions of childhood needs were enmeshed in the need to administer childhood because of growing concerns about child abuse.

Child abuse gave a renewed impetus and importance to child needs. The need to administer children where there were concerns about safety also produced expert commentaries on motherhood. Motherhood was formulated in ways which made it possible to "deal" with mothers through a particular apparatus which was connected with child protection, and not hygiene and population control, which were some of the ways of dealing with bad mothers in the nineteenth century. Child abuse gave us the "bad mother," and the need to speak about bad mothering gave us the "good mother." Thus motherhood was rendered in administrative terms. The good mother is an administrative invention in child abuse narratives, the means by which the bad mother is identified and reformed. Without the bad mother she would not exist: there would be no need to "fix" her qualities in narrative terms; she would remain un-commented upon, shrouded in silence. And linking the good mother with the cause of child rights has put her beyond the reach of even feminist critique, since no-one supports harming children. Indignation rightly raised by spousal abuse has carefully negotiated the ways in which women were positioned in relation to child abuse as victims. So firmly cast as victims were women in the early feminist imagination, that even when mothers were perpetrators they were cast as "victim-perpetrators" (abusing because they were once victims themselves). The bad mother simultaneously invents motherhood and rescues it from feminist critique.[1]

The bad mother also occupies a symbolic position in mothers' lived conceptions of themselves. Mothering work is made up of the minutiae of small decisions and actions taken in specific contexts, often privately, hastily, and very much "on the job." In the reflexivity which comes with this way of working, mothers enter into dialogues with themselves and others about "how they are doing." This is especially evident in conversations between mothers about mothering work. In this dialogue popular/professional conceptions of the bad mother occupy a strategic position. In positioning themselves between "goodness" and "badness" mothers are constantly scrutinizing their practice for clues about their success and failure. The bad mother acts as a means of self-appraisal and reflexivity; she is a yard-stick and an informal regulator of individual mothering behaviour.[2] Social categories like good and bad mother are not external to the individual; we may accept or reject these categories on an individual basis. But in doing so we are forced to negotiate with them. This enforced negotiation is one of the social consequences of rendering motherhood in these administrative terms.

The narratives surrounding motherhood are numerous. Phoenix, Woollett and Lloyd (1991:1-2) have pointed out that the psycho/social academic literature on motherhood can be divided by genre. First, there are the development psychology texts which stipulate what mothers should be doing for children. These ideas filter through into popular ideas. Second, there are the "how to" manuals which give endless practical advice on dealing with (mostly small) children. Third, there are the research studies which look at motherhood as a major life transition point. Fourth, are the auto/biographical accounts which review motherhood as an experience. Finally, there are the feminist texts which analyze motherhood as a dimension of women's lives and a key element of feminine identity. The sociologically-oriented narratives on motherhood are now dominated by feminist scholarship, and it is this diverse genre which best contextualizes the concerns raised in this book.

Feminist scholarship has attempted to excavate motherhood from a kind of "natural history." By releasing motherhood from arguments about human nature and social function, feminists have pointed to the mythological underpinnings of motherhood, and to its convenience as a social arrangement, variously serving the social, economic, and political agendas of hegemonic male and/or capitalist interests. These intellectual endeavours have been accompanied by a political rhetoric suggesting that by somehow disembowelling motherhood, women's lives can be reclaimed and personal autonomy won. Motherhood has always occupied an ambiguous position in feminist thought: it is both a major site of female oppression and a voluntary living arrangement which permeates all dimensions of social organization. Motherhood, for many feminist researchers, is an unpalatable fact of social life.

The political rhetoric of feminism collapsed into the private introspection of lifestyle politics in the early 1980s in North America and Britain. This collapse was graphically illustrated for me because it corresponded with a particular time in my autobiography. I left Britain in 1981, newly armed with my Ph.D., to teach sociology in a university in Nigeria. I left a thriving women's movement dealing with women's rights in reproduction, education, law, medicine, and so on. But when I returned two years later there remained only a political rhetoric with no organizational base. The women with whom I had worked on a range of issues were to be found in one of two places: in therapy, or camped out at the American missile base at Greenham Common — the last public expression of British feminist politics. With this shift in politics from public to private came a paradigmatic shift away from criticizing capitalism and patriarchy and toward two newly formulated concerns: fragmentation[3] (indexed in cultural representation) and the regulatory mechanisms involved in the construction and maintenance of motherhood as a social category. We will explore some examples of the feminist writing concerned with fragmentation and regulation and so establish some of the conceptual ground of this chapter.

Fragmentation

Kaplan (1992) highlights recent shifts in the representation of motherhood in popular culture. Kaplan's is a postmodern cultural studies framework which stresses instability, negotiation, ambiguity, fluidity, and contingency (key concepts in the postmodern lexicon) in place of social structure and certainty.[4] Kaplan argues that there has recently been a fragmentation around motherhood which is responsible for changing the ways in which we understand it. She argues that in the late 1980s and early 1990s motherhood (and fatherhood) has been newly located as an uncertain and transitional role in lived culture. In these new uncertainties surrounding traditional family roles we glimpse "the possibilities of new female subjectivities" (ways of being) as dispersed, multiple, unstable, and in process (Kaplan 1992:219). Kaplan is suggesting that this period brought a greater flexibility — evident in academic and popular narratives about motherhood — in which we see some important changes. There is, she argues, a greater acceptance that mothers will be working. There are important acknowledgements that mothers occupy diverse social positions in which black and poor mothers face particular difficulties. Race and class become important axes of fragmentation around motherhood, whereas previously the psychological dilemmas of the white middle class had been held up as the universal "motherhood experience" (Kaplan 1992:190). Fragmentation

acknowledged that many more social identities were available to mothers and that important social changes had occured in women's lives.
This kind of analysis is helpful in recontextualizing motherhood in
contemporary terms as a dynamic set of lived experiences and relationships.

The political conclusion of this analysis — that it was the prospect
of fragmentation and diversity which rescued women from their subor-
dination — is problematic. First, because women occupy a greater
range of social positions we need not assume that gender disadvantage
is less of a problem. Fragmentation is a helpful analytic tool; it is not a
political solution. Indeed, fragmentation greatly complicates the task
of political mobilization as it is harder to appeal to a constituency
which is highly conscious of its differences. Second, it is not clear how
the multiplicity and flexibility of public images of motherhood actually have an impact on the lived experience they acknowledge. Multiple
subjectivity and identity for mothers are held in check by certain features of the political, administrative, and organizational structures in
which identity and subjectivity are organized. The accessibility to, and
ability to afford, day-care provision, women's employment opportunities, and their levels of pay all importantly structure the available (lived)
range of motherhood identities. No mother, however much she believes
it is possible, is about to become an astronaut without some very good
support networks and affordable day-care. There is no explosion of
motherhood identities: only a slow seepage which needs support and
social provision. Third, working motherhood was not recently accepted as a new "identity opportunity." Non-working motherhood has only
ever been a choice for the privileged, and working motherhood is now
de rigueur in households where there is an expectation of two incomes,
and especially for mothers forced to live on welfare who are being tar-
geted as a major drain on public resources (Nathanson 1991:59-72). In
my own, limited, experience of mothering over the last twelve years (in
Britain and North America) urban professional women with young
children have shifted from justifying why they work, to justifying why
they stay at home.

Finally, political and theoretical fragmentation came much earlier
than Kaplan suggests, at the end of the 1970s, and was initiated by

women of colour, lesbians, and trade union women objecting to the racial and class politics of the organized women's movement.[5] Motherhood has, arguably, always been a transitional role in lived culture and it has always been the site of multiple identities. What held this multiplicity in check were the intellectual and political frameworks through which we encountered motherhood, and not motherhood as a lived experience. It was structuralist and modernist frameworks which could not cope with multiple identities, not women (and men) themselves. Historical accounts of women's lives are full of ambiguity and multiplicity. Violet Trefusis and Vita Sackville-West, for example, admittedly privileged women, conducted an open lesbian relationship and travelled alone quite freely in the heart of British society in the 1920s and 1930s (See Nicholson 1992). What has changed is the conceptualization of motherhood in academic narratives and the development of a political rhetoric and practical interventions which aimed to reposition women in society. This change is connected not just with the emergence of postmodernist frameworks, but with the theoretical and political vacuum left by the collapse of the organized women's movement at the end of the 1970s. Fragmentation offers no political program; the best it can do is assert individual rights to lifestyle difference and hope that this promotes social change. [6]

Regulation

Seeing the family as the outcome of the many forms of discipline and regulation which operate around it and give it shape clearly draws upon the framework of Foucault and Donzelot discussed in Chapter One. Consideration of the forms of disciplinarity and regulation shaping modern motherhood has made a major contribution to its conceptualization in recent social analysis. The social regulation of mothers, via an insistence on the specific requirements of children, forms the substance of disciplinarity in feminist writing. Many writers quite properly highlight the connection between motherhood and the requirements of childhood stipulated by developmental psychology and psychoanalysis, implicitly developing childhood as a key site in the regulation of motherhood. Phoenix, Woollett and Lloyd (1991:1-2) argue that developmental psychology has failed to properly address motherhood in its focus on the requirements of children. Dally's (1982) account of motherhood as a recent, idealized invention organized by a set of demands made on behalf of children by "experts" pursues a similar argument. The same point, with detailed attention to post- war theories of maternal deprivation developed through the popularization of child psychology, is made in Riley's (1983) *War in the Nursery*. Riley effectively captures the intellectual and social policy climate in which the modern mother-child bond was conceptualized, at least in Britain. She argues that this bond occupies a central position in statements about mental health and the quality of the social fabric. Although the connection between the quality of motherhood and the prosperity of the nation was an old (eugenic) and not a new theme in the post-war period (Hooper 1992), it was newly underpinned by psychological and psychoanalytic enterprise which offered expertise on childhood.

The project of exploring motherhood through its regulatory mechanisms is, perhaps, more explicit in Carol Smart's (1992) edited collection *Regulating Womanhood*, which contains Valverde's interesting discussion of the Ontario Dionne quintuplets.[7] This collection of essays explores the gendered forms of regulation operating through socio-legal discourses around motherhood, sexuality, and marriage. Carol-Ann Hooper's (1992) discussion of child sexual abuse in 19th-century Britain resonates with earlier versions of this book in noting the regulatory effects of medicine and mother-blaming in child abuse (Knowles 1991), an insight developed from Donzelot's (1979) account of the early alliance between motherhood and medicine in the regulation of family life.

This kind of work, situating motherhood within its regulatory mechanisms, makes an important contribution to a general understanding of how motherhood was construed as a social category through its central ideas and apparatuses. But it does have limitations. It deals mostly with the macro and the hegemonic levels, so that the forms of contestation and plurality of meaning which are invoked around motherhood remain hidden. Examination at the micro level of social agencies and their narratives at least gives a sense of how hegemonic notions of motherhood are asserted, and it gives a sense of the multiplicity concealed by hegemonic notions of motherhood. Another of the limitations of social regulation frameworks is that they perpetuate the theory that women themselves exercise only minimal forms of social agency. The social roles making up motherhood are always defined by the requirements of others: children, society in general, the social projects served by disciplinarity and regulation, capitalism, men, and so on. Women do not feature in this formulation as conscious social agents making decisions about their lives.

The narratives excavated for the multiple meanings of motherhood in this chapter, like the last with its concern to understand childhood, are the practice-oriented narratives of academic pediatricians, psychologists, public health workers, and psychotherapists. What distinguishes these narratives from the output of academic feminists on motherhood is their attention to the practices of child protection and their concern with the multiple forms of "pathology" associated with motherhood.

The Centrality of Motherhood

In this chapter I will argue that motherhood is given an analytic and practical centrality in narratives concerning child abuse. Reviewing the professional narratives of child experts it becomes clear that the quality of motherhood is the key to defining, identifying, and managing many forms of family "pathology," including child abuse. Motherhood is the central object of professional narratives concerned with child abuse. This centrality is obscured by some professional narratives which effect a gender neutrality. The shift from "mothering" to "parenting" appears at first to be an important admission of the social responsibilities of mothers *and* fathers, but as soon as the content of "parenting" comes under closer scrutiny in the narrative it becomes more gender-specific and "mothering" re-appears in place of parenting. The most obvious example of this is Leventhal, Fearn and Stashwick's (1986:72) discussion of the "parenting" abilities of "mothers," which goes on to discuss "disorders of parenting" and how they are detected in "maternal behaviour." This slippage is a common feature of professional narratives. Turner (1982), in a study done for the Ontario Health Ministry, uses "parenting" in his title and then switch-

es to "mother" throughout the text. Clearly the reduction in the use of
the term "mother" does not mean that mothers are any less central in professional narratives concerned with child abuse.

The switch to gender neutrality pays lip service to feminist concerns: it is a superficial form of "political correctness" which is not sustained in practice, in the ways in which people think about motherhood, or in the ways in which motherhood is administered. My point about the significance of mothers in professional narratives is better established with examples later in this chapter.

Motherhood does not simply occupy a central position in the daily drama of family life in professional narratives. As the primary carers of children in our society, mothers are held responsible for child abuse (Institute for the Prevention of Child Abuse 1990:4) either as perpetrators or by indirectly failing to protect children from the abuse of others. Evidence of a limited retreat from "mother blaming" is found in some of the official Canadian federal and provincial reports on child abuse. This shift is partly a result of changes in the ways in which these reports are construed. The Report of the Special Advisor to the Minister of National Health and Welfare (1990), for example, unlike many of the reports commissioned by the Federal Family Violence Prevention Division of Health Canada, does not pursue the customary discussion of who abuses and why. It is in these discussions that mothers are most clearly implicated as responsible for abuse. The report of the Special Advisor focuses instead on the identification of abuse by "reading" the child for signs. It focuses on preventive measures involving research and inter-agency co-operation and action around child advocacy. In this way child abuse is cast as a social problem requiring an apparatus for detection and management, and not as a problem of individual family or motherhood failure. This is a small shift, but it implies a movement in emphasis from motherhood to childhood, and from individual blame to systems for detecting and dealing with family failure. Whether this position is sustained in practice or, indeed, what it *means* in practice is more difficult to assess. A more progressive approach would be to generally unburden motherhood with extensive state provision of day-care, as is found in France, where a high proportion of children over two have a day-care place.

Dichotomizing and Judging Motherhood

The tendency, noted in earlier chapters, to distinguish high-risk or dangerous families from a norm by constructing two discrete populations, is a distinction premised on mother-child interaction. Mother-child dynamics are a major site in the judgement of motherhood and in the assessment of the whole family. This is particularly the case in psychological and public health narratives, though it is not necessarily a distinction used in child protection narratives. Schindler and Arkowitz's (1986:247) laboratory-based assessments of the nature of mother-child interaction divides "subjects" into "physically abusive mothers" and "matched non-abusive" mothers, used as a "control." The control group then operates as a norm against which the psycho-social profiling of abusive mothers can generate them as a "type." There are many investigations of this type sustaining different kinds of pathological-normal distinctions (Lovett 1995; Ethier, Lacharité and Couture 1995). The general thrust of this kind of investigation is to determine what mix of social and psychological traits goes into the psycho-social pathology of the (exotic) "abusive mother." Implied exoticism acts as a distancing mechanism in which the "normal" seek to understand the behaviour of the bizarre. Schindler and Arkowitz's research is based in Tucson and published in the mainstream American *Journal of Family Violence.*

The division of mothers into these two seemingly discrete populations — "abusive" and "non-abusive" — implies no recognition that this categorization might be contentious. Instead it implies that this demarcation is taken-for-granted knowledge by the professionals to which mainstream psychological research findings are directed. The mothers in each category in Schindler and Arkowwitz's research were identified from the caseloads of child protection workers and therapists, a fact which implies some level of professional collusion with the validity of this categorization:

> Normal control subjects, obtained from preschool, also were briefed.... Over the course of eight months, 11 abusive mother-child pairs agreed to participate. All of these mothers had been

identified by caseworkers or therapists as being physically (or in one case, exceptionally emotionally) abusive to at least one of their children in the last 6 months. Each family had been involved with the State of Arizona Child Protective Authorities.(Schindler and Arkowitz 1986:249-50)

"Abusive" in this case means under the surveillance of child protection authorities, and "normal" means a mother whose behaviour is not subjected to agency scrutiny. The definitions of abusiveness used by child protection agencies also implies a level of collaboration between psychological and social welfare and psycho-therapeutic narratives. We know, from narratives on dangerousness in Chapter Two, that assumptions around social class and dependence on welfare play a significant part in allocating people to problematic and non-problematic populations. Leventhal, Fearn & Stashwick (1986:76) also discovered that as far as medically based judgements were concerned, pediatric residents regularly made good parent/ineffective parent judgements (of mothers) based on "in- office" observation of behaviour. This finding indicates that the effective presentation of self and compliance with professional directives may be a key element in the judgement of mothers by a range of professionals involved in child protection.

The assessment of motherhood, at least in some professional narratives, seems to be an arbitrary and precarious business. This arbitrariness is worrying, given the very serious consequences which can follow the assessment of motherhood as inadequate. The removal of children, extensive agency surveillance, the use of legal instruments to regulate family life, and so on, are all possible consequences with far-reaching implications in people's lives. The kind of professional certainty represented in Schindler and Arkowitz's (1986) work in identifying good/bad, abusing/non-abusing mothers may well endanger the children of the good mother. The good mother is rescued from stigma by the identification of the bad mother as problematic; the good mother's child-rearing practices are hence placed beyond question and surveillance.

Good mothering remains a largely implicit norm in professional narratives about bad mothering. Good mothering is the implied standard against which pathology is indexed, but it is rarely directly discussed. Good mothering surfaces as an explicit set of capacities only in certain circumstances: around direct attempts to identify and reform bad mothering. Self-help initiatives, organized under the rubric of public health in major Canadian cities in which good mothers are used as role models for bad mothers, provide us with an example of these circumstances. Toronto has a number of these public health schemes, including a scheme called "Parents Helping Parents." Here good mothers are "intelligent" and have a good "knowledge of infant needs" (Conference Presentation, 1990, Institute for the Prevention of Child Abuse, Toronto). It is this that they offer as support and leadership for mothers identified as placing their children "at risk." Other attempts at reforming mothers come from specific "treatment" programs such as the one documented by the Parent and Child Therapy Society (1984) in Vancouver, which draws upon the experience of a similar scheme in the United States.

The other circumstance in which the good mother surfaces is in the assessments of mothering made around childbirth, under the auspices of perinatal medicine. Gray, Cutler, Dean and Kempe's (1976) work on perinatal medicine is linked with the pioneering work of Helfer and Kempe on child abuse in the United States. Perinatal medicine attempts to identify the bad mother during her hospital stay, and these early observations have provided a model for other initiatives in perinatal medicine. Gray's (1982) *Welcome Baby Manual* is intended to guide the assessments of hospital nursing staff in identifying early problems in mother/child interactions. Here the good mother has "the ability for tender, empathic, individualistic, prompt, and predictable care giving. ... better parenting [means] more attachment behaviours, and lessened child abuse" (Gray 1982:141). Being a good mother is a matter of "attitude" and "social circumstances": the baby is wanted and planned (Gray 1982:3), and the mother is socially and emotionally "effective" in her home and understands the "optimum growth and development" of her children (Ledger and Williams 1981:41). She also has a "repertoire [127] of child oriented skills": she can "comfort the child," she can be "consistent without rigidity." And she knows how to "avoid some power struggles" (Parent and Child Therapy Society 1984:34). The good mother also lives in "positive family circumstances" (Gray, Cutler, Dean & Kempe 1976:378). This involves an appropriate support system, "stable" living conditions, a husband who has "a stable job" and is "supportive." According to the Toronto self-help scheme "Parents Helping Parents," not only does the good mother have a stable family background, she also has impressive skills in household management and organization. Sent in as missionary agents of change to work with the reformable sections of an underclass of bad mothers, good mothers ultimately bring order and domestic management to otherwise chaotic lives. The good mother lives in the Parsonian middle-class nuclear family of the 1950s: a two-parent family in which there is a clear gendered division of labour and role complementarity. A good mother does not require the intervention of social agencies herself; rather, she can be mobilized as a community resource in the project of social reform.

These qualities of good mothering, perinatal medicine insists, can be "read" in the quality of the bonding process. As Gray (1982:142), citing Kennell, Voos and Klaus (1976), says:

The affectional bonds a mother and father establish with their infant during the first days of life are crucial for his future welfare. When the bonds are solidly established, parents are motivated to learn about their baby's individual requirements and adapt to meet these needs: they are willing to change diapers thousands of times, to respond to the baby's cries in the night, and to provide stimulation appropriate in intensity, time and quality. Fully developed specific ties keep parents from striking their baby who has cried for hours night after night — even when they are exhausted and alone.

Of course, good mothering is not a matter of professional consensus. The conceptions of perinatal medicine and public health departments are not necessarily those of child protection or family therapy. I do not even want to suggest that the good mother is a matter of consensus *within* the professional boundaries of perinatal medicine or public health. The views I cite, however, have a hegemonic hold on research and writing concerned with child abuse.

A rather different view of the good mother is posed by the Parent and Child Therapy Society. This is a more psychoanalytically informed and child-centred model which also incorporates some rather moralistic judgements about housekeeping. With the aid of a checklist in which every item begins "Does the parent..." (otherwise referred to as "she"), the Parent and Child Therapy Society presents the good/bad mother in the same list of behaviours:

- Does the parent feed the child foods which are appropriate to the age and individual needs of the child and family budget?

- Does the parent determine what the child should eat, according to an idiosyncratic belief system, which reveals the parent's distaste for messy food or high expectations of the child's development; ie will not allow a night bottle because the child is 2 years of age, will not serve foods which result in sticky hands/face....?

- Does the parent show disgust regarding bodily functions of the child...?

- Does the parent dress the child in a manner which is appropriate to the normal activities of the child's age/stage of development?

- Does the parent allow the child to explore indoor/outdoor environment — by the provision of suitable toys/equipment, opportunity?

- Is the child's bedtime appropriate to age/development of the child or to serve the interest of the parent?
  (Parent and Child Therapy Society 1984:33)

This conception of the good mother is less rooted in the Parsonian

nuclear family and more closely under the explicit direction of psycho-　
analytic experts in children. The good mother here is the mother who
is prepared to keep her practice open and under review so as to absorb
the advice of experts on the delicate and ever-expanding nature of child
needs.

Bad motherhood

Professional narratives concerned with child abuse generate a repertoire of bad mothers. "High risk mothers," "psychologically maladapted mothers," "negligent mothers," "devious mothers," and "dangerous
mothers" are some of the different dimensions of bad motherhood to
be featured. These different interpretations of bad motherhood are
partly to do with different kinds of child abuse, e.g., psychological,
physical, and sexual, all of which raise their own particular mothering
pathologies. Negligent mothers are obviously more associated with
child neglect than dangerously violent mothers, who are associated
instead with physical abuse. This repertoire of bad mothering is also
partly connected to the different professional concerns and practices of
the agencies involved in administering child abuse. Psychologists, for
example, may be more interested in maladapted motherhood than, say,
child protection workers who focus on dangerousness. These mothering pathologies also correspond to administrative designations organized through research into abusive parenting. These research projects
discover and affirm certain ways of speaking and thinking about mothers. These ways of seeing mothers have some important social consequences.

What it is like to be a mother described by these categories of bad
mothering is quite a different matter. The distinction between administrative categorizations construed by agencies and researchers — dangerous mothers, maladapted mothers, and so on — in order to deal
with what are seen as social problems, is likely to be quite distinct from
the existential or experiential dimensions of bad motherhood construed by individuals. I refer to this distinction between professional
and individual (insider) narratives in order to make the point that there
is no necessary connection between the two. Life-story narratives told

by black schizophrenics show that populations defined as problematic in a psychiatric sense live around, through, and in opposition to, administrative designations of who they are (Knowles 1994). In other words, "problematic" people themselves do not simply absorb professional narratives about who they are and what their problems consists of. This is a point missed in social constructionist accounts, but it is a point which will be evident when we consider stories told by members of abusive families later in this chapter.

High-risk motherhood

Our preliminary discussion of risk in Chapters Two and Three indicated that risk was a strategy for the identification of dangerousness. The bifurcation of the family into its dangerous and benign forms organized a conception of childhood as endangered, and offered it as a target for social management. The endangered child is endangered precisely by the high-risk mother.

Dangerousness is not about the total quality of family life; it is unevenly focused on the behaviour of mothers. But risk has a circuitous relationship to motherhood: it is rarely the case that mothers are held directly responsible for child abuse in professional narratives; they are commonly more closely associated with neglect. This denial of responsibility for abuse, in fact, draws mothers into the centre of the family frame. Mothers *are* held responsible for child care and for the overall quality of family life, and the management of abuse in the home is therefore firmly situated in the mother's domain. Mothers, rather than fathers, are certainly a target for professional intervention and reform. The gender of parents responsible for sustaining a high risk situation in The Parent and Child Therapy Society's (1984) attempt to socially locate an abusing population is revealed in a description of a single parent:

> In those families where neglect coexisted with abuse, the socio-economic profile usually differed. The profile would then more commonly be:
> Single parent — sometimes with a succession of *males in the home.* [author's emphasis]

Welfare recipient.
Chaotic lifestyle — poor housekeeping standards.
                  — no routines for child care.
                  — alcohol or drug use.

Since housekeeping, child care, and relationships with men are pre-dominantly associated with women, it is safe to assume that this is a profile of a high-risk mother rather than a father.

The target of risk assessment in perinatal medicine is also inevitably the mother/patient. Bonding is most commonly applied to an analysis of the mother/infant relationship rather than father/infant relation-ships:

American society approaches the task of bringing up children with considerable ambivalence. We cannot seem to decide how seriously to take the idea of a science of child rearing. From blam-ing mother for the child's every developing characteristic, we move to recognizing that mother's needs affect the baby and that we therefore must be non-critical of her. From a heavy handed dissemination of new research indicating that certain modern conveniences — anesthesia, bottles, formula — are not as good for baby as the old fashioned ways, we shift back to a recognition of the social, financial and political stresses women suffer and a consequent letting up on mothers. And now to the latest discov-ery that even in the earliest moments of life, the mother-infant relationship is critical. (Gray 1982:138-9)

Ledger and Williams' (1981) classic *Parents at Risk: An Instructional Programme for Perinatal Assessment and Preventive Information*, pro-duced for the British Columbia Ministry of Health and approved by the Registered Nurse Association of British Columbia, provides a practical and influential guide for medical staff on maternity wards who are involved in the business of risk prediction. At the centre of Ledger and Williams' argument is the same claim that maternal behaviour around delivery has good predictive value for risk detection. They cite research on the maternity charts of fifty abused children which apparently

FIGURE 1   PARENTS PHYSICAL AND PSYCHOLOGICAL
                                      WELL-BEING

PREGNANCY	pregnancy is perceived as very difficult or burdensome mother feels her health will suffer from childbearing or childrearing mother intellectually sub-normal shows great depression over pregnancy mother remains feeling frightened and alone, especially before delivery. Careful explanations do not dissipate the fear excessive visits for health care or expresses multiple psychosomatic complaints evidence of emotional instability or mental illness history of drug or alcohol abuse child wanted in order to fill unmet need in parents' lives evidence of low self-esteem (I'm no good") particularly re parenting ability mother aged under 20 previous pregnancy has resulted in abortion, fetal or neonatal death, or birth of damaged child history of previous child's death or removal from home due to abuse/neglect
LABOUR AND DELIVERY	mother experiencing excessive discomfort, fatigue, drug effects or physical complications immediately following delivery mother and /or father perceive labour and/or delivery as very traumatic or unsatisfactory obvious lack of supportive interaction between couple hostile interaction between couple
POST PARTUM (K. Ledger and D. Williams (1981) An Instructional Program for Perinatal Assessment and Preventive Information. Ministry of Health, Province of British Columbia.)	mother does not see attention focused on infant as something positive for herself mother bothered by infant's crying; makes her fell helpless, hopeless or unloved mother relinquishes control to doctors and nurses for meeting needs of infant evidence of low self-esteem ("I'm no good"), especially re parenting ability parents express excessive feelings of failure re performance during labour/delivery parents express resentment/anger toward infant over childbirth experience express excessive doubt re ability to care for infant

CHARACTERISTICS OF THE CHILD	PARENT-CHILD ATTACHMENT
	pregnancy unplanned or unwanted parent(s) considered abortion or relinquishment denial of pregnancy, i.e., unwilling to gain weight, refusal to talk about pregnancy in advanced pregnancy dresses and acts as though she is not pregnant absent or disturbed response to quickening mother perceives fetal movements as abusive or aggressive actions mother reports an experience she fears will damage baby (i.e., a "scare", accident, etc.) undue concern re infant's sex or performance absence of any fantasies about what the baby will be like or predominantly negative fantasies mother attributes negative characteristics to fetus apparent lack of concern for the physical well-being of the unborn fetus, as evidenced by a refusal to make health and lifestyle changes (i.e., poor nutrition, excessive use of drugs/alcohol, etc.) absence of "nesting" behaviour in the third trimester (i.e., preparation of clothing, equipment, space for infant)
premature physically or mentally defective immature or defective reflex behaviours unresponsive condition necessitates separation from parents "wrong" sex looks and/or behaviour perceived in negative way by parents	mother look distressed, disappointed does not talk to infant in affectionate terms makes negative or hostile remarks to infant expresses disappointment with sex of infant mother makes inappropriate verbalizations, glances or disparaging remarks about or toward infant avoids eye contact and direct "enface" position mother doesn't hold, touch ore examine infant mother handles infant in rough manner
as above perceived by parent as being different or "not normal" despite negative findings sex of infant remains unacceptable to parent denies or exaggerates handicapped infant's capabilities difficult feeder unresponsive, i.e., sleepy baby irritable or difficult to console hyper reflexive rigid or non-cuddly	does not comfort infant when crying and does not heed physical needs appear apathetic toward or disinterested in infant express excessive doubt about ability to care for infant remain disappointed over sex of infant frequently voice negative feelings about or toward infant repelled by messiness and diaper changing negative identification of infant by name or association with someone disliked no feelings of attachment toward infant after one month mother does not appear to enjoy playing with infant

showed that in twenty-two cases there were comments by concerned nurses in the post-partum period about the "mother's ability to cope with her infant's physical and emotional needs" (Ledger and Williams 1981:84). Ledger and Williams take their list of warning indicators from Gray (1976)(see Figure 1).

Although some of the warning indicators of risk are based on the interaction between the parents, they are predominantly focused on the mother's behaviour toward her infant, and scrutinized for forms of bonding failure. The absence of "nesting behaviour," looking "distressed," and "inappropriate" responses to the new infant are all grounds for suspicion. "How does the mother look?", "What does the mother say?", "What does the mother do?", "Does she have fun with the baby?", "Is she passive or hostile?", "Is she negative or bothered by crying?", "Does she avoid eye contact?" (Gray 1982:1-1) — all of these things become significant in the maternity ward, where they are importantly interpreted by psychological and social profiling. Gray (1982:1) also lists depression, lack of social support, denial of the pregnancy, having considered an abortion, coming from an abusive or neglectful background, and living in "crowded" or "unstable" conditions as conducive to risk. Responsibility for child care is extended to include responsibility for non-care: neglect and abuse and bonding becomes the bio-social site of pathological mothering.

We noted in Chapters Two and Three that risk had an epidemiology, a social distribution among populations, which was organized by notions of social class in which the poor were especially stigmatized (Martin 1985:53-64). The epidemiology of risk is also importantly structured by gender, in that motherhood and fatherhood are differently implicated in its narratives. Mothers have a less direct relationship to causing abuse, but a more direct social responsibility for its detection and management as this and the next chapter will show. Child protection workers work predominantly with mothers. Callahan's (1993:68-73) case studies illustrating the nature of casework all involve work with mothers. Social workers say they work with mothers more than fathers not because they hold them more responsible for the quality of child care in a family, but because it is the mother who is most often available to be dealt with.

The idea of identifying risk is clearly connected with tracking with [*135*] community resources an identified population of new mothers leaving hospital. It is about targeting resources where there is most need. Public health schemes operating in the City of Toronto and which claim to deal with risk are the "Healthy Beginnings Project," "Parents Helping Parents," and the "Healthiest Babies Possible Project." I am not contesting their claim to deal with risk, but these schemes do not, I suspect, share a notion of risk with child protection workers. The missionary dimensions of the "Parents Helping Parents" project, mobilizing good mothers to reform the bad, was discussed earlier. The other two projects are aimed at "super high risk women" (Conference Presentation, 1990, Institute for the Prevention of Child Abuse, Toronto); and whilst those who organised these schemes were hard pressed to say exactly what they meant by "super high risk," the projects' connection with food banks, and concerns about nutrition and the distribution of milk tokens clearly equate risk with poverty and mothering in less than ideal circumstances.[8]

But the risk of a socially disadvantaged childhood is not the same as the risk of severe neglect or abuse. Child protection workers, for example, place a good deal of emphasis on risk assessment. Their assessments of risk have a broader timescale than the brief snapshots of perinatal medicine. In the Matthew Vaudreuil case in British Columbia,[9] the enquiry into Matthew's death refers to the *Family and Child Services Manual* used by social workers in British Columbia to assess risk:

A risk assessment is the systematic collection and evaluation of information relevant to determining the ongoing risk to a child within the present living arrangements...
- age and vulnerability of the child
- extent and severity of injury/neglect
- previous reports of unexplained injuries or chronic, severe neglect
- parental ability to admit responsibility and use support services
- ability of non-abusing parent to protect child
- availability of family support
- the child's ability to protect himself

- the parent's mental or emotional condition
- the home environment
- family dynamics, and
- the reliability of the information of reporters or collateral as factors to be considered.

(Report of the Gove Inquiry into Child Protection Vol.2:70-1)

These risks are then balanced against the parent's strengths in coming to a decision about the real extent of risk in a family. (Unfortunately in this case there was a general agency failure to protect Matthew, who was killed by his mentally sub-normal mother.)

Child protection workers generally have an operational notion of risk. Yet such a notion is a calculation and not a statement about disadvantage, and it stresses the severity of neglect or injury and the social context supporting that neglect or injury. Child protection calculations of risk may less clearly implicate mothers than the narratives of public health and perinatal medicine. This is in part because child protection deals with family dynamics in their home context and not on a medical site for a limited period of time. With an emphasis on inter-agency dialogue and co-operation also comes the prospect that sometimes agencies are talking past each other, as may be the case in the differences between perinatal/public health conceptions of risk and child protection notions of risk. The concept of risk in motherhood is elastic, and it is further explored by examining the other constructions of bad motherhood with which it overlaps.

Psychologically maladapted motherhood

The psychological profiling of the bad mother is a pervasive narrative which seeps into many different kinds of professional narratives with different priorities and focuses. Psychological profiling generally occurs around attempts to understand why abusive mothers abuse. It is also used in an effort to identity and reveal those who are likely to abuse: high-risk mothers. The psychologically inadequate or maladapted mother has a repertoire of personality failings which typically included neediness, depression, anger, aggression, and anxiety (Ethier, Lacharité and Couture 1995). In offering a checklist of neediness and personality [137] failings which have a bearing on the capacity to mother, the Parent and Child Therapy Society (1984:34), for example, suggests that professionals check the number of statements that parents make concerning the incompleteness of their lives, e.g. "cannot live without the child" or "needs the child to give her a purpose in life."

The depressed mother, too, makes frequent appearances in professional narratives, establishing maladaptation, as this researcher from Michigan State University reports:

> The depressed mother has been described as rejecting, harsh and punitive in her attitude towards her children. She uses frequent physical punishment, or is listless and neglectful. Elevated risks of depression have been found among mothers of pre-school age children, the group at highest risk for abuse and this effect is exacerbated in single mothers.(Seagull 1987:44)

Psychological "maladaptation in the mothering role" is also commonly linked with "anger aggression" and "anxiety" to give an "overall psychological distress score" (Turner 1982:9). Reporting on the published psychological investigations of other American and Canadian researchers, Turner reports:

> There is considerable evidence that the experience of emotional distress may matter importantly for maladaptation in the mothering role.... The goal that guided this aspect of the study was to contribute towards development of more effective procedures for distinguishing mothers who are at elevated risk for parenting problems. (Turner 1982:9-13)

The psychopathology of maladapted motherhood, then, can be measured or "scored." Mothers, like children, function as indicators of malfunctioning families. But unlike children, they are held to be the central players in family malfunction: family failure is the personal failure of the mother. In the cases cited in this section her failure is located in psychological and personality terms.

Psychopathology does not stand alone. It typically invokes a narrative considering its social context as Seagull's comments on single mothers suggest. A typical social context would include a lack of social support, high geographical mobility rates, and transitory lifestyles (Seagull 1987:44-5; Adamakos, Ryan and Ullman 1986:464-9). Adamakos *et al.'s* Ohio-based research aligns a psychopathology of mothering with various social measures. These include the "Maternal Support Index," the "Parenting Stress Index," and the "Inventory of Home Situation," all of which are deployed in order to align psychological profiles with social factors:

> ...the majority of the follow-up mothers were unmarried and unemployed, had less than high school education. and were on public assistance, (e.g. welfare, food stamps and/or ADC). (Adamakos *et al.* 1986:464)

Maladapted motherhood is part of a constellation of psycho-social pathologies. But ultimately, scientific-sounding measures, diagnoses, and personality types point at the same group of poor women whose lives are organized by systems of social welfare. The University of Western Ontario psychologist David Wolfe (1985:6) is critical of the psychological quest for the maladapted mother:

> ... the results indicate that studies using measures of underlying personality attributes or traits have been unable to detect any patterns associated with child abuse beyond general descriptions of displeasure in the parenting role and stress related complaints.... Abusers did not differ on any dimension from members of other problem families.

Maladapted mothering covers a range of behaviours and many variations in the degree of risk, from less than attentive care to the highly dangerous. Because of this range it has no serious predictive value in indicating child abuse. The concept of the maladapted mother offers, in psychological terms, the profiles of women whose emotional economies and lifestyles need monitoring and management so that they

are not harmful to children. On one level this is true: we cannot sepa- [*139*]
rate the emotions of mothers from the quality of mothering.
Mothering is a highly emotional job. But the concept of the maladapted mother offers a false sense of security that there are only "certain
types" of mother whose affairs need to be monitored. These are the
same "types" who are likely to be poor and living on welfare and whose
affairs are over-scrutinized anyway because they lack other options.
The concept of maladapted motherhood sustains an inherently conservative political agenda. Instead of encouraging the unburdening of
motherhood with day-care provision so that the psychological capacities of mothers become less important, this kind of research encourages an additional reason for scrutinizing an already scrutinized population of women. Nor does this aid the task of child protection,
because the family affairs of those who are not identified in terms of
psychopathology may be seen in too positive a light. This optimism
may cause experts to overlook certain families, ones in which children
may have lesser standards of protection because their family behaviour
does not arouse professional suspicion.

Negligent motherhood

Negligence is another of the range of administrative meanings attached
to bad mothering. It has a long historical precedent which is evident in
discussions of the slovenly habits of the nineteenth-century poor in
Canada in the context of the social reform (Ursel 1992:70-4) and the
moral reform movements (Valverde 1991:129-142). But negligent motherhood has been transformed by its association with child abuse. Child
neglect, along with non-accidental injury, was one of the early concerns
of the 1960s. Negligent motherhood implies a deliberate strategy of
absence and a calculated ineffectiveness. It is a passive, rather than a
malicious attempt to cause harm, and is most often established in narratives about "adequacy" in child care. This passivity is congruent with
one of the key themes associated with femininity in cultural narratives.
   The negligent mother is not only foregrounded in child neglect but
also, more recently, implicated in sexual abuse. The negligent mother in
sexually abusing families is characterized as accepting deviant behav-

iour from partners and spouses, and is frequently characterized as powerless and ineffective in her family (Dawson 1982:91). Strand (1991:378) refers to the large number of research reports detailing ineffective and negligent mothering as a variable in sexual abuse cases. In the shift from neglect to sexual abuse, negligence takes on a new set of meanings and forms of psycho-social pathology. Mothers have moved from being directly (if passively) responsible for abuse to being indirectly responsible. Dawson (1982:91) notes that "Some mothers are aware [that their children are being sexually abused]. ...these mothers fail to limit the behaviour of their spouses."

Negligent mothering is hence a failure to manage the violent or sexually predatory behaviour of men.

But negligence also has another meaning: it is about abandonment of the family, about being "literally or psychologically absent" (Dawson 1982:91). In the vacuum this creates around family sexuality in which "both the father and the daughter realize that the mother has deserted them" (Henderson 1972:92, cited in Dawson 1982), the mother implicitly and tacitly bequeaths sexual matters to her daughter. Negligent mothers in incestuous families are often characterized as "frigid" keeping "themselves "worn out so as to limit their sexual availability" (Henderson 1972:93, cited in Dawson 1982). Hence negligence in this context has two meanings: it is a failure to limit male behaviour and it is an abdication of sexual responsibility in the family. The normal mother, by implication, manages the sexual economy of her family rather more effectively. This firmly links motherhood with the management of the sexual economy of the family.

Negligence has its own forms of psychopathology. Negligent mothers are frequently characterized as "passive, dependent personalities with a low sense of esteem who are deprived of self fulfilment within the family." They may also be "lacking in social skills, isolated and psychologically and financially dependent upon their husbands," as well as being "emotionally immature" (Dawson 1982:91). It is these psychopathologies which render mothers powerless within their families so that they fail to "protect their child" (Henderson 1972:108, cited in Dawson 1982), and fail to manage family sexuality. Negligence is a construction of motherhood which accords motherhood limited forms of human agency. These mothers are so passive that they are not capa- ble of asserting themselves enough to be dangerous. The negligent mother fails to properly assert her central place in the family, a place which is by implication, a feature of normal motherhood.

The negligent mother is the most closely associated with a failure to protect her children from sexual abuse in professional narratives. This mother explains why she did not leave her husband when she discovered he sexually abused their daughter. There is no sense from her story that she sees herself as negligent.

> I was not in love when I married, but I grew increasingly fond of my husband over the years. Before my marriage I used to think I was in love, but I seemed always to pick someone who drank too much or wasn't in love with me. Then I deliberately picked someone to marry who I thought would be acceptable to my parents, who had a bright future — and who I thought would be a good father. I was wrong on the last premise.
>
> My husband abused me and the children verbally, and he sexually abused my oldest daughter, his step-daughter, from the time she was eight until she was eighteen — which I only recently discovered when she was hospitalized for serious depression.
>
> I wanted to leave him, but we have been together for thirty two years and I feel guilty about leaving him now, as he is ill. Also we really don't have enough money to live on separately.
>
> He has done some really bad things in our married life. He forced me to have four children when only two were planned. He insisted I had to have a hysterectomy when it wasn't really necessary.... (Hite 1994:50)

This story certainly sets out some of the complications surrounding why mothers stay in abusive families. For this woman, but possibly not for others, the abuse of the daughter was outweighed by the longevity of her relationship to her spouse and the other benefits which came with this, such as financial security. We see here also the commitment to stay together and the guilt which would come from leaving. We also see — and this is fiercely debated in professional narratives — that this mother did not know (or cannot admit) that her daughter was being abused. This mother does, however, see herself in terms of a narrative of victimization in which her abusing husband is all-powerful, and in which she is powerless. In this she supports some of the professional and official government narratives regarding the gendered nature of social power. In the case of this woman power differentials are deployed to justify her decision to stay in an abusive relationship. Professional narratives can be deployed in personal explanations; they have many uses and social consequences.

Devious motherhood

Devious mothers are more proactive than negligent mothers. They are able, for example, to mobilize the social assumptions concerning the sexually predatory nature of masculinity to their advantage. The meaning of motherhood as deviousness emerges from various places. One of these is the Sexual Abuse Legitimation Scale developed by Gardner (1987), a clinical professor of child psychiatry at Columbia University. This is an instrument which claims to be able to identify genuine from fabricated sex-abuse claims. It is used to help establish "truth" in custody and access cases that are judicially contested, and where claims of sexual abuse made by the mother are suspected of being made in order to deny paternal access to children. Indicators of deviousness in this scale include a vengeful attitude toward the partner, a lack of shame over the abuse, the retention of a lawyer or a mental health worker as support, attempts to corroborate the child's testimony and a failure to appreciate the importance of children's maintaining a relationship with their father.

> Very valuable differentiating criteria...
> Initially denies or downplays the abuse.
> If the complaint was not made in the context of a child custody
>   dispute or litigation, check yes...
> If she does not want to destroy, humiliate or wreak vengeance on
>   the accused, check yes...
> If she has not sought a "hired gun" attorney or mental health

professional, check yes...
    If she does not attempt to corroborate the child's sex abuse
        description in joint interviews, check yes... (Gardner 1987:6)

In other words, any competence shown by the mother in handling the professional apparatus which coheres around child protection is interpreted as deviousness. What is appropriate or normal behaviour by mothers in these circumstances? Helplessness?

The implication of this kind of narrative is that mothers benefit from accusations of sexual abuse; they use this accusation to manage fathers, something which negligent mothers are accused of not doing. Mothers who are forced to unleash the apparatus of child protection to prevent further sexual violation of their children are scrutinized, judged, and tortured by its investigations. Their child care practices are the subject of scrutiny and reports prepared by child protection services, by the police, by psychologists, by psychiatrists, and by school teachers. And ultimately, much of this investigation of mothering detracts from the question of whether or not the father is guilty of abuse.

I am guided in these comments by a story that a woman in London told to me. Her accusations of sexual abuse aimed at her partner (whom she was convinced was sexually abusing their son) were seen by the father's lawyer as part of a move to prevent the father from seeing his child. The father was wealthy and had a good lawyer; the mother lived on welfare. It took several years for the mother to piece together the fact that her partner was abusing her child, and when the child disclosed the abuse she took steps to prevent all future unsupervised contact with his father. The court case in which the father sued for access to his son took several weeks, and in the months leading up to it the woman and her child were subjected to extensive agency investigation and reporting of an intrusive and upsetting kind. She was psychologically assessed and began to doubt her own capacities as a mother, which she felt were on trial anyway. In court she was frequently reduced to tears by her partner's lawyer. But when she finally broke down in court and confessed that the whole process of the trial and the investigation surrounding it had made it impossible for her to mother her son at all, that she went home from the court "in pieces" each day, the judge stopped the proceedings. In the negotiations which followed, her partner withdrew his claim for unsupervised access — a tacit admission of guilt. Most interesting was the behaviour of the police. They had been convinced all along that the child was telling the truth, that he had been abused. And they did concede that there was a question of public interest here: the man could abuse other children. But, they said, they would not press charges because the man had a psychiatric history, which made it difficult for them to secure a conviction. It took the woman a year to recover from the trial and the investigations surrounding it. Many times she wanted to give up, but she knew that if she did her son would go on being abused by his father. It will take the child years in therapy to recover from what has happened to him.

Dangerous motherhood

Constructions of motherhood as dangerous contest the negligent, the devious, and the maladjusted, all of which support the location of motherhood within dominant public images of victim-hood and passivity.[10] It is in some ways quite odd that those who are socially accorded a centrality in dealing with children (including disciplining them) should at the same time be absolved by some, but not all professional narratives, of any direct involvement in physical and sexual abuse. There is an obvious contradiction here between dominant public images of women as being both passive and primarily responsible for children. There is also an evident ambiguity about the extent to which mothers exercise forms of human agency. They are only held indirectly responsible for child abuse; theirs is a failure to protect. And yet they are a central object of professional intervention and social reform of family life.

Evidence of a more direct role in child abuse by mothers has been available for a long time and is only now being re-read. Greenland's (1978) classic and much cited *Child Abuse Deaths in Ontario*, for example, gives brief case studies of families in which child abuse deaths have occurred. Many of the cases directly implicate mothers as being responsible for fatal abuse. The early studies by Finkelhor *et al.* (1979)

on sexual abuse noted, but offered little comment on, the extent of sex- [*145*]
ual abuse among boys, some of which implicates mothers. Citing an
old (1965) U.S. study, a psychologist working for the Toronto Youth
Services commented at a national conference on child abuse that
"Canadians are turning a blind eye to thousands of cases of child abuse
committed by women and girls, and as a result are failing to provide
treatment for boys who may grow up to be rapists..." (*Globe and Mail*
30 October 1991:1). These and other findings challenge the traditional
gender dynamics of child abuse narratives. Clearly mothers can be dangerous too.

Jill Korbin's (1987) qualitative life-story approach to understanding
mothers convicted and imprisoned for fatally abusing their children
throws little light on the meaning of dangerousness. This is because she
does not use the life-story approach to discuss any dimension of dangerousness with her interviewees. Instead, the social context of lethal
mothering is construed from the usual textbook list of risk factors
(Korbin 1987:405). Like other researchers before her, she mines the
usual site of pathology: problematic mother-infant bonding. In doing
so she finds periods of mother-infant separation, maternal perception
of the child's development as "abnormal" or even "possessed," and
"rejecting" and "difficult behaviour" (crying) in children (Korbin
1987:405). To this she adds scenarios of stressed social and psychological circumstances to complete the context of lethal mothering. In
terms of prediction and understanding, then, there is little to distinguish dangerous mothering from other problematic forms of mothering. In terms of child protection there is a case to be made for being
able to identify dangerous mothers. But if lethal mothering cannot be
distinguished from all the other forms of bad mothering, some of
which are quite benign, what could possibly be the rationale for the
measurement and judgement of motherhood in these terms? What is
the political agenda here?

Generally, however, there is a resounding silence in professional narratives over the relationship between motherhood and the use of violence in child-rearing. We may gain some sense of this relationship,
however, from personal narratives. Here is a statement about a mother
by her child. It sets out some of the contradictory feelings the (now

adult) child has about her mother. It also reveals something of the ways in which the mother managed her interactions with her children.

> My mother was very loving but punished me often — usually verbally, but also by hitting me. I had a love-fear relationship with her. It was rather confusing.... She would control me by yelling, hitting and using the Bible against me, which she knew I believed in. She would harp on the verses of submission of children to parents, and of women to everyone... (Hite 1994:35)

The use of physical as well as verbal discipline by mothers on children is not uncommon, but it is not usually publicly discussed. In a 1990 survey in Britain conducted by *Woman's Own* magazine, 90 per cent of the respondents admitted to smacking their children, although 50 per cent regretted doing so (Hite 1994:42). Given this kind of evidence, mothers routinely smack children as part of "normal" mothering.

Compared to men, women have cornered the market when it comes to producing narratives of what it is like to experience life in abusing families. But most of these narratives are concerned with women as the objects of abusive relationships, either as children or as adults. There are few stories in which women themselves discuss the more violent and abusive elements of their mothering. Most of the stories about violent mothers are told by the children of these mothers. The following story is told by a street kid in Toronto:

> I remember one time in particular that the social workers came. I was about eight. About a month before, a kid in my class must have guessed that I was real hungry because he took me home. When his parents saw the shape I was in, they kept me for a week but I guess they didn't call the cops or nothin'. When I went home, she beat me very bad, then locked me up for weeks until some friends of hers called the CAS, but they never did nothin', never took me away. I don't know why, maybe because of the show she put on when they came. She didn't go any easier on me as I got older. Well, she did change — got rougher, started beating me with a whip. (Webber 1991:22-3)

Those mothers who do confess to being violent toward children do so in the context of their own history of violence as children, thus offering their own childhood as explanation. This is an implicit collusion with the victim-perpetrator relationship established in many professional narratives. It again makes the point that people appropriate professional narratives to tell stories about themselves.

Victimhood, Youth, and Poverty

Victimhood, youth, and poverty are some of the more generally significant narrative themes organizing the meaning of "bad" mothering. The focus on the poor has already been noted. The Toronto "Healthiest Babies Possible" project characterizes its target "high-risk" group as low income, new immigrants, and smokers, living in poor housing conditions with weak social-support networks and low self-esteem. The victimhood status of mothers is secured in asserting their predominantly indirect relationship to child abuse, and in subsuming them within the violent family as though they occupied a similar place to abused children. Even dangerous mothers are conceptualized historically as victims of abusive situations as children, thus maintaining a victim analysis for the victimizer. But mothers, unlike children, have effective powers of negotiation and alternatives to violent family life:

> Young mothers are also seen as inherently problematic. Adolescent mothers and their offspring are a high risk group both psychologically and emotionally. Poverty, malnutrition, complications of pregnancy, emotional problems such as depression, drug and alcohol use, are all risks for the mother. Children [of these mothers] are also at greater risk for cognitive and emotional problems. (Hechtman 1989:569)

This is really part of a broader narrative about teenage sexuality and its social consequences in physical and emotional health, and in economic and social status. These are issues which Constance Nathanson (1991) deals with in the current context of the highly racialized welfare politics of the United States. Hechtman claims that there are elevated rates of mental defectiveness in the children of adolescent mothers. She also believes, evidently, that intelligence is racially distributed.

> Lower intellectual ability has been reported in children of adolescent mothers not only early in life but in childhood and adolescence. Children of adolescent mothers in a black urban population had lower intellectual scores [this psychiatrist obviously has no qualms about either the definition of blackness or intelligence, whether the tests actually measure intelligence, and whether they make assumptions about culture] at ages eight months, four years and again at seven years in comparison with a matched sample.... There are also considerable adverse effects in the social and emotional development of children of adolescent mothers. These children have difficulty adapting to school and have more learning disabilities than children born to older mothers.... Younger mothers also tend to be slower in responding to the baby's needs ... younger mothers are less emotionally close to their children and provide less intellectual encouragement...(Hechtman 1989:572)

This is a severe condemnation of young mothers across a broad range of social, economic, developmental, emotional and racial factors from a very authoritative source: at the time of writing Hechtman was the acting head of psychiatry at the Montreal Children's Hospital, Quebec's main medical facility for children. Narratives which implicate poverty, adolescence, and race in the social construction of bad motherhood attach child abuse to a range of other social problems, and to populations widely construed as inherently problematic on several levels. This points to an underclass of mothers associated with a range of psycho-social pathologies.

The mother as victim and the cyclical nature of victimhood are recurrent themes in insider accounts of motherhood. In the following account, Sylvia Fraser, a Canadian adult survivor of child sexual abuse, tells the story of her wedding day.

As the organ swells, I see my shadow intensify. That shadow is the last thing I see, for it is not I who arrives at the altar but my other self, fastened to her daddy's arm, dragging her muddy train of memories down the aisle like a cat with dead rats tied to its tail.

"Dearrrly beloved, we are gathered in the sight of God and of man..."

I will have no memory of the wedding ceremony. It will never be written on my consciousness any more than a band inscribing water produces a record. If it hadn't been for the photographs, I would never believe I'd been there.

"Who gives this woman?"

"I do"

I will have no memory of the wedding night. Sexual initiation is the territory of my other self. She-who-would-not-wear-white has been summoned to stand fierce guard over her own secrets. (Fraser 1987:140-1)

This is a story of victimhood which stresses the intense psychological disturbance of which some professional narratives warn. Another woman, from a Pennsylvania shelter for abused women, speaks of the effects of her own physical abuse at the hands of her husband — and, in the past, her father — upon her behaviour toward her own children. Hers is one of a minority of stories by a mother admitting violent feelings toward their children, though it is contextualized by her own victimization in the manner I described earlier:

> I could grab him [the baby] right now, if he did something bad, and throw him up against the wall.... My dad used to do that to me, now I may do it to this kid. (Ferrato 1991:54)

This story confirms the "cycle of abuse" stories told by professionals. The cycle, like the concept of victimhood, foregrounds the helplessness of women and their lack of human agency.

But in many personal narratives there is also evidence of resistance: of women who make a decisive break with their personal past and reconstruct their lives and their child-rearing practices:

When Faith and Bob brought their newborn son home, Bob played the proud Papa and quickly learned how to change diapers. It seemed as though the bad times were behind them.

A year later, however, I got a letter from Faith saying that the marriage was over. She wrote that Bob hadn't been able to stop trying to control her: he had taken up his old violent behaviour again. "The baby and I have moved to our own little house," she wrote. "I'm learning how to be a single parent — we are actually quite a contented family. When Bob comes into the picture the story changes. He has been a never-ending source of trouble. I had to get a restraining order against him because he would not leave me alone. I had a friend over one night, and Bob was outside watching us through the window." (Ferrato 1991:87)

Mothers who tolerate violence themselves frequently pause to consider how it affects their children (Langley & Levy 1977:116). They escape with their children (Hoff 1990:35) so as also to escape the social consequences which come with abuse. Mothers also make calculations concerning violence, as this woman suggests:

I felt trapped with the kids, he had the money, he threatened to hurt the kids if I left.... Sex was a strong contributing factor. I used sex to control ... to punish him, to prevent battering, and to prove my worthiness.(Hoff 1990:44)

Although this woman's partner controlled the money and the threat of physical violence, she still used whatever resources were within her control to contest his actions and assert a kind of power of her own. No-one is powerless, and women, too, harbour violent fantasies:

I came this (she gestures with her hands) close to killing him with the machete.... He escaped to the bathroom ... I didn't kill him because I knew they would take me away and my kids wouldn't have anyone.(Hoff 1990:53)

Narratives recounting personal experiences, then, reveal a little of the complexity of the power and sexual dynamics in families. Where there is abuse, mothers have an ambivalent and contradictory relationship to violence within the family; they also have a complex relationship to power, even those who fear the physical violence of their partners. There are some points of convergence between professional and personal narratives, especially around violence and victimhood and the ways in which mothers hold themselves responsible for the care and safety of their children. And there are also some significant points of divergence between professional and personal narratives, specifically around naming and categorization, which make up the administrative inventions of motherhood. Personal narratives do not use the concepts of good and bad motherhood explicitly: they have no need to because they do not need to turn motherhood into an object of administrative action. They deal with motherhood by living it.

Conclusions

The construction of good and bad motherhood as oppositional forms organized by narratives on child abuse provides an opportunity to fine-tune motherhood as a practical activity in professional narratives. It is an opportunity to let all mothers know what is expected of them. The distinction between good and bad mothering itself is a disciplinary mechanism which impinges on the practices of all mothers. We are all good or bad depending on the way we live, the stories that we tell about our family histories, the psychological profiles we reveal, and the behaviour which we model under professional surveillance.

Although notions of good and bad are organized by conceptions of class, poverty, race, and gender, they are by no means clear-cut distinctions. Good and bad motherhood are dissected by contradictions and ambiguities of meaning established in different professional narratives and practices. Negligent mothers fail to manage fathers and the sexual regime of the family effectively. Devious mothers over-manage fathers and fail to demonstrate appropriate helplessness around professionals. High-risk mothers fail to demonstrate the appropriate emotions around their infants. And maladapted mothers highlight women's emotions as targets for social management. In each case good mothering is implicitly or explicitly construed in opposition to bad mothering so that these two administrative categories keep shifting places. The terms in which motherhood is rendered in professional narratives also impinge on the ways in which mothers see themselves and tell stories about their lives.

There is no obvious coherent political agenda attached to these administrative processes, although they do invoke new forms of social management around women at some very intimate and private levels in their lives. This management through motherhood places some real constraints on the multiplicity organized around female identity referred to by Kaplan (1992), and makes the point that not all forms of multiplicity are empowering. Some kinds of multiplicity simply render women additional targets for social management and reform: processes in which other women (good mothers and social workers) play a significant part as agents for social change. In theoretical terms motherhood is caught in a conceptual "crack" between a multiplicity of meaning and strategies of social management.

In the end we have to live with the fact that childhood and motherhood are, in fact, construed as oppositional categories in social management strategies around child abuse. The effective protection of children is a violation of the rights and freedoms of mothers whose public identities are severely constrained by the demands made on behalf of children by experts. In order to manage child abuse motherhood is rendered in the terms described in this chapter. But need it be so? Do the terms in which motherhood is rendered offer effective protection to children? Or do they merely make life more difficult for mothers without actually improving child protection?

1. While much feminist writing is critical of "wifedom" very little is openly critical of motherhood. Feminist attention to motherhood is limited to arguments for a more socially defined responsibility for family matters in the provision of daycare and a more equitable re-allocation of responsibility for children between mothers and fathers.

2. These comments are based on my own experience of mothering and the many conversations I have had with other mothers over the years — a kind of participant observation.

3. I do not intend to suggest here that what took place was just a collapse of feminist rhetoric. There was also the collapse of a more general feminist politics which had played a part in securing a range of significant improvements in women's lives, from shifting public images to equal pay and opportunity and reproductive rights. Much of this had dissipated by the early 1980s as a more or less cohesive movement with an action based form of political engagement.

4. For a discussion of postmodernism see Zygmunt Bauman's (1992) *Inimations of Postmodernity* (London: Routledge).

5. The fragmentation of feminist politics was spearheaded by women of colour in Britain and the United States, and in Canada by Native women too. Their claim was that feminist politics was dominated by the concerns of white middle class women who were involved in various forms of racism excluding and disadvantaging black and Native women. See Caroline Knowles and Sharmilla Mercer (1992), "Feminism and Antiracism: An Exploration of the Political Possibilities," in James Donald and Ali Rattansi (eds.), *Race, Culture and Difference* (London: Sage) for a summary of these arguments. The voices of Canadian Native women on these issues is to be found in the *Journal of Canadian Women's Studies* (1989), vol. 10 nos. 2 & 3.

6. Caroline Ramazanoglou (1992), "Feminism and Liberation," in Linda McDowell & Rosemary Pringle (eds.), *Defining Women* (London: Polity) makes an attempt to mediate between the politics of identity involved in fragmentation and the need for a form of feminist politics to address women's concerns.

7. See Mariana Valverde (1992), "Representing Childhood: the Multiple Fathers of the Dionne Quintuplets," in Carol Smart (ed.), *Regulating Womanhood*. Valverde (1992:119) makes the interesting point that the Dionne quintuplets were constructed and displayed as representations of "childhood," that they were no more "children than Mickey Mouse is a mouse."

8. This is not intended to deny the importance of dealing with poverty in public health interventions. The problem comes in identifying poor people as high risk for child abuse. This is not supported by research and is unnecessarily stigmatizing.

9. See the Report of the Gove Inquiry into Child Protection in British Columbia (1995).

10. This is not an argument for mothers to be conceptualized as being equally dangerous as men. But there is a case to be made for being more open and not covering up female violence with dominant images of femininity. Only then can we consider more fully the extent and nature of child abuse.

ADMINISTERING FATHERHOOD

FATHERHOOD, like motherhood, is the site of multiple and contradictory meanings in the professional, practice-oriented narratives which deal with child abuse. What is most striking about professional narratives is the marginality of fatherhood. While professional narratives are replete with references to motherhood, references to fatherhood are so scarce they have to be found with a magnifying glass and interrogated for every nuance. Hence the range of meanings "invented" around fatherhood are highly restricted in comparison with motherhood. It emerges that motherhood and fatherhood, not surprisingly, are construed in terms of quite distinct relationships to the family, to childhood, and to the abuse of children. In this respect there is a convergence between professional narratives and popular conceptions of motherhood and fatherhood, and there is also, to some extent, a convergence between these and personal narratives. In this chapter we are concerned with the ways in which fatherhood is rendered in professional narratives.

Fatherhood as an Object of Social Analysis

The marginality of fatherhood in professional narratives concerned with the detection and management of child abuse is no longer reflected by a small amount of academic publications on the subject. Fatherhood and the more general area of masculinity have become items of growing interest in social analysis over the last ten years. But despite growing interest, fatherhood has not been given as much attention as has motherhood.[1] Jackson (1984:9) notes that this imbalance is "an index of our knowledge." But it is more than this. The absence of fatherhood is also an index of social relations and attitudes, of forms of cultural representation, and of the nature of intellectual production and its gender relationships.

Academic production around the family in which fatherhood was traditionally marginalized is bound up with the ways in which the family was seen as a site for investigation. The family was broadly conceptualized as a female domain in early sociology, in part through the efforts of developmental psychology, which gave a scientific validity to the "natural" mother-infant bond. The family belonged to women just as the work belonged to men. Jackson (1984:9) suggests that the problem is the "sovereignty of motherhood" over the domain of the family, and the fact that much of our empirical research data on the family is derived from mothers, with fathers not having found a "voice" in family matters. But it more than a question of fathers' silence on family issues. The gender relations of the family as a site for investigation also secured it for female academics. The private world of the family and its domestic relations, in contrast to the serious investigation of the macro-social processes of work, organization, and social structure, became the intellectual territory of women researchers. The family was thus investigated in particular ways, ways which explored the experiences and work of mothers but not of fathers. The family was "left" for women as a marginal domain in sociology, and it appealed to women because a large part of their lives was organized and represented through it. The family, of course, is intimately connected with the public images of femininity. Female academics themselves had a marginal relationship to intellectual production and the prestigious university posts which came with it. Hence a marginal area of research became the intellectual property of a marginalized group of researchers. The privileging of mothers over fathers in the intellectual production of the family is therefore tied to the history of the development of sociology and its internal gender relations. And these gender relations are themselves tied to the organization of the academic labour market.

If the story of fatherhood was not written, it is because those who might have written it had other concerns: concerns which were tied to prestigious research grants and academic posts. Those who complain that fatherhood has been written out of social science literature (Lamb 1983:4; Franklin 1984) might pause to consider why fatherhood was so recently "discovered." As Ginsburg (1991:358) astutely observes, the story of fatherhood has been obscured by the history of men. Men's roles as fathers were obscured beneath the larger and more important public roles assumed (historically) to be the domain of masculinity. The omission of fatherhood in social science literature is therefore the product of the social privileges of masculinity, and as such is hardly grounds for complaint.

The gender relationships of the family as a research site are connected with the broader, gendered, relationships of societies. It is this connection which many analysts see in presenting the family as a site privileging the rights of mothers over fathers (Franklin 1984). The claim that mothers have won a package of rights in relation to children, which is denied to fathers (Lamb 1983:2), has led to attempts to redefine fatherhood in more active terms. These attempts parallel the more active legal attention being paid to fathers in child custody and access cases on both sides of the Atlantic. The concern (which emerged in the mid-1980s) to explore and reposition fatherhood represents a shift in the importance attributed to the family as a research site and as a living arrangement. It also reflects some important shifts in the gender relations of intellectual production in which women academics are making progress by moving into domains previously dominated by men.

Masculinity and Fatherhood

As an object of intellectual enquiry, fatherhood is contextualized by some of the more recent studies of masculinity. These studies are worth reviewing for the theoretical insights they offer the investigation of fatherhood as a social construct. The study of masculinity allows us to think about fatherhood in terms of its social and emotional conditions of acquisition, its maintenance, and its broader cultural scripts (Weeks 1986:65). Masculinity is not a given, but a site of contradictory meaning and context:

They [the concepts masculinity and femininity] are fraught with conflicting and contradictory messages, and they have different meanings in different contexts. They do not mean the same thing in formal social documents or legal codes as they do in popular prejudice. They mean different things in different class, geographical and racial milieux.

And yet whatever the qualifications we make, they exist not only as powerful ideas but as critical social divides ... to power differentials and to historical situations where socially and practically men have had the power to define women.(Weeks 1986:59)

The conditions under which masculinity is acquired also involve the negotiation of plurality, or different ways of being male. Like femininity, masculinity it is not a unified concept. The different versions of masculinity — masculinities — in play in any society have different relationships to power and to social sanction and legitimation (Morgan 1992).[2] Not all masculinities are equally socially sanctioned. Morgan (1992:97), for example, uses "hegemonic masculinity" to describe the ascendancy of dominant social images of masculinity, and the process by which these images are sanctioned and legitimated. Hegemonic masculinity is also a term Connell (1987:184) develops, inspired by Gramsci, to describe "a social ascendancy that extends beyond concepts of brute power into the organization of public life and cultural processes." Hegemonic masculinity is hence an ascendancy embedded in social practices. It is offered to explain why some versions of masculinity — tough macho images, for example — gain ascendancy over other versions of masculinity, such as homosexuality.[3]

Masculinities are not "given" cultural scripts; they are generated by the ways in which we live. And masculinity is not just learned through socialization; it is "worked-up" through the "gendered encounters" of everyday life (Morgan 1992:203). In the social relationships of the workplace, for example, gender relationships are performed on a daily basis in the interactions between (male) managers and (female) secretaries, or (female) students and (male) professors. I watch the performance and acquisition of masculinity and femininity on a daily basis as I watch the male professor whose office is close to mine deal with his female students: the ambiguity, the playing on familiarity and distance, displays of authority and flirtation, the negotiation of grades, the performance of different degrees of power. Ways of being male (and ways of being female) are generated and acquired through the concrete social practices and social relationships which make up the fabric of everyday interactions of individual and social life.

This theoretical framing of masculinities applies also to fatherhood. Fatherhood has a plural set of possibilities, with hegemonic and subordinate forms associated with it. Fatherhood is also a multi-version social construct, generated and acquired in the practices and interactions of the everyday conduct of fathering activities. It is a set of ongoing possibilities which men live out according to their notions of themselves as males, according to the constraints of the situations in which they father, and according to the ways in which they negotiate living space with other family members. Fatherhood, like masculinity, is framed in different social policy contexts and arenas. And it is framed in particular ways in narratives concerned with child abuse — the focus of this chapter.

Masculinity and Violence

The relationship between masculinity and violence occupies a central place in the narratives of masculinity, fatherhood, and child abuse. The central question being addressed is this: Are violence and sexually predatory activity deeply embedded in the social organization of masculinity and fatherhood?[4] There are two answers to this question, both of which have a bearing on the issues in hand: the first is that masculinity is inherently violent; the second is that violence is not inherent but embedded only in certain forms of masculinity. It can, therefore, be deliberately acquired or rejected as a way of being male and as a way of fathering. We will take a closer look at these arguments, beginning with the first.

Arguments locating violence and predatory sexuality as a key element of male identity tend to favour an account of masculinity as inherently violent. Kuypers (1992:28, 64) makes this point quite convincingly, arguing that the "global nature" of male violence invades all human situations, from the most intimate to the most organized, because violence is a key component of male identity. Lethality, he insists, is embedded in masculinity, embedded in its "everyday actions" which are organized by the "codes of violence" governing male behaviour. Kuypers then goes on to support his argument by discussing the research findings locating men as perpetrators of different forms of family violence, including child abuse. He offers two explanatory models for men's relationship to violence. The first is the social control theory, which argues that in the absence of social sanction men will behave violently because they get away with it. The second is the model favoured by feminists and by official federal and provincial government reports on child abuse and family violence in Canada. This is the theory that male violence is simply the inevitable, negative consequence of patriarchal power. Both theories really amount to the same thing: societies support male violence. This assertion, problematically, invokes a macro- and not a micro-political agenda. It is the nature of social structures which have to change according to this argument and not male behaviour. This argument invokes an ambitious project of social reform which also relieves men of the responsibility for moderating their behaviour.

Hearn's (1990:66) support for Kuypers' argument proceeds along a different route than male identity. Hearn argues that males are inherently dangerous because of the violence embedded in the social construction of masculinity, although he doesn't explain the mechanisms by which this takes place. In rightly contesting the failure of agencies to address fathers in their management of child abuse, Hearn suggests we have failed to explore the place of violence within "normal masculinity." Fatherhood, he contends, is organized by its history and by its social relationships, both of which are embedded in violence. Indeed, fatherhood in most social analyses is intrinsically problematic:

> paternal authority is routinely oppressive [in its] routine avoidance, denigration, insulting, ignoring and putting down of young people by fathers, which is seen as a legitimate part of being a father [and which] accumulates to child abuse. (Hearn 1990:70-6).

In this analysis it is masculinity which is the problem and which needs reconstruction, and not society as a whole. The advantage of this over Kuypers' account is that it offers violent masculinity as a more manageable target for social reform.

Contesting the thesis of inherent male aggressivity is the theory that violence is socially acquired along with masculinity. Weeks (1986:65) argues that fatherhood, like sexual identity and sexual difference, is constantly being construed and reaffirmed and acquiring meaning in lived culture. Rape, domestic violence, and child abuse are therefore not about an "inherently aggressive masculinity" but about the "social and psychic conditions in which masculinity is acquired ... [in] complex social practices and psychic structuring."

Morgan (1992) concurs with this conclusion that men are not inevitably connected with violence. Although violence may be sanctioned by the dominance of cultural imagery connecting it with maleness, violence is only one way to father and to be a male in any society. There are other strategies and choices to be made. This analysis puts the onus on male behaviour and challenges fathers to re-examine their ways of relating to their partners and to their children. Male behaviour, as well as its social context, is surely a target for social reform.[5]

We now turn from theoretical frameworks to a more detailed discussion of some of the ways in which fatherhood has been conceptualized and reinvented in academic narratives tracking the emergence of "new" forms of masculinity. The "new man" was the conscious construction of the mid-1980s, and was a bid to usurp the traditional domestic terrain which many mothers had been trying to renegotiate with fathers. The challenge issued by, and on behalf of the new man to rethink the nature of masculinity was organized in a social climate which ostensibly favoured gender equality in the home and especially in the area of child care.

Reinventing Fatherhood

The construction of the new man was intended to increase men's involvement in child care and domestic responsibilities. It is hard to establish the extent to which fathers participate in these activities. We do know, however, that single fathers are massively outnumbered by single mothers. In 1991, the proportion of families in Canada headed by a lone male parent was 2.3%, compared to 10.7% headed by a female lone parent (Vanier Institute of the Family 1994:7). This in itself is a statement about the positioning of fatherhood in relation to major responsibilities for children. The reinvention of fatherhood around new meanings and practices also reflects significant social changes in the lives of women. And it most especially reflects the increased labour-force participation of women with young children. There are many sightings of the "new man" as the reinvented father in the 1980s. He makes an appearance in McKee and O'Brien (1982) and in Bronstein (1988:3, 254), who speaks of the "new father" of American media and popular construction — the father who is involved with children.

> Judging from the flurry of articles in the popular media over the last five years on "the new father," it appears that new roles and options for parents have become a fact of modern-day life. These articles present examples of men and women sharing in house-work and child care — sometimes with the men taking over the larger share — in homes where both parents are in the labour force, and moving forward in the career of their choice. Thus the message seems to be that with some careful arranging of sched-ules, and some initial effort in the early years to find some good day care for their children, both fathers and mothers can experi-ence satisfaction in their work life and a rich and rewarding fam-ily life. This family life is seen as one in which fathers are just as likely as mothers to stay home when their infant is sick, or go to a teacher conference, or take their 12-year-old to the orthodon-tist, and in which spouses experience a deepened sense of respect, equality and co-operation with one another.(Bronstein 1988:3)

The new father is thus associated with the "good life." But Bronstein shows that this popular media construction is only partially lived out in real families. The new father is also being consciously and deliber-ately created in academic forums, examples of which can be found in a number of articles in *The Journal of Contemporary Human Services*.

And then there are attempts to "celebrate" fatherhood: Bowman's (1993:22-27) account of the three-generation "Father-Son Project" in the United States is an attempt to insert active fatherhood into the concept of normal masculinity. In this project fathers highlight attributes such as demonstrating love, passing on legacies between father and son, paying attention to father-son relationships and dealing with the "wounded child within" (Bowman 1993:25). This is clearly an attempt to stake out the need for male emotional health and intuitiveness.

The "new man as active father" in the American literature is also ethnicized. Bronstein's (1988) collection contains chapters on the "Black Father" and the "Chicano Father" as though they were distinct sub-species of the fathering population. And maybe they are in terms of public imagery and representation, though surely not in terms of behaviour. McAdoo's (1988:79) "Changing Perspectives on the Role of the Black Father" addresses those studies which assert that black fathers have a negative impact on family life, concluding that black fathers show child-rearing attitudes and involvement in line with those of other ethnic groups. The African-American father is thus reinserted from the margins of social pathology into the domain of the new man as active father.[6]

Old and new: centre and periphery

Arguments about old and new masculinities and the models of fatherhood which they sustain are really about the relative peripherality and centrality of fathers within the family. Different narratives give conflicting messages about the social positions occupied by fatherhood. The new man may be seen as an attempt to reinsert men into family responsibilities which were previously thought to belong primarily to mothers. But what is really *new* about the "new man as active father" is difficult to establish. The idea that something is being reinvented is premised on the assumption that radical changes have occurred in fatherhood as a series of practical day-to-day engagements, and not just a shift in narrative gears. This is complicated by our lack of understanding of the nature of fatherhood as a practical activity both today and in the past. The historical models of fathering that we are using as a yardstick by which to measure change, themselves contain inventions of fatherhood in terms of a set of "traditions" which may or not match the ways in which lives are lived.

In terms of historical traditions of fatherhood we have Donzelot's (1979) account of the alliance between the bourgeois mother and medicine in the management of the eighteenth-century family in France to guide us. We also have his account of the inducements to working-class men to abandon the public spaces of the taverns and the streets and place themselves under the maternal authority of home and hearth. Both of these moves construed as specific and marginal the contributions of men at a crucial historical point in the "shoring-up" of the modern family. In these accounts men were "dealt" out of family life in terms of child care and the domestic domain. But Donzelot's is an analysis focused on the impact of public and social policy on the management of the family in the greater task of national efficiency. It gives us little sense of how fathers actually lived and behaved toward their children.

There are other historical narratives which give a better picture: fragments contained in marriage contracts and family settlements, in family photographs and portraits, in tax records and parish registers, and in diaries and memoirs. All of these sources contain hints about how men have responded to the challenges of fatherhood (McKee and O'Brien 1982:13-14). Paul Thompson's (1977, cited in McKee and O'Brien 1982:19) work on oral evidence drawn from five hundred men and women in the British census of 1911 showed that parent-child relationships varied enormously. His oral history of the family points to the complexity of looking to the past for uniform models of fatherhood.

Mirroring the obscurity of past versions of fatherhood, there is surprisingly little discussion of the detailed practices and living arrangements which make up the new man version of active fatherhood. This is clearly an area for empirical investigation. There are attempts to differentiate fatherhood from motherhood in terms of content and process, but these are rather vague. Garbriano (1993:51), citing Margaret Mead, suggests that fatherhood is more ambiguous than motherhood and relies less on cultural prescription: "Fatherhood has

no givens," and in some children's lives it is an "anachronism." [165]
Fatherhood is also frequently discussed in terms which suggest it is
more active than motherhood. Pruett (1993:46-51) highlights the nurturing dimensions of fatherhood and the "active, vital and vigorous"
babies produced by active fathering which are "loved more dangerously" (a reference to Erikson). None of this is new. It is a version of
fatherhood traded routinely by the experts who acknowledge that
father-child interactions differ significantly from mother-child interactions. Some fathers spend less time caretaking but engage in physical
stimulation and unpredictable play which infants often prefer (Rutter
1984:145).

Arguments about old and new versions of fatherhood and concerns
about the centrality and peripherality of fathers in family affairs pose
some serious problems concerning the relationship between narrative
and practice. It is hard to know whether fathers were traditionally edited out of the family as a lived experience, or whether they were simply
edited out of the texts which documented the family — in sociology, in
history, and in psychology. These texts tells us as much about the organization of sociological, historical and psychological narratives as they
do about the societies on which they were offering commentaries. It is
not entirely clear whether the emotional dimensions of fatherhood
were eclipsed by the marginality of fathers in children's lives, or by their
marginality in the narrative productions documenting children's lives.
Jackson (1984) could well be addressing both dimensions with his plea
to fathers to enjoy their children at the expense of other more public
social roles. Further evidence of practical involvement of fathers with
children is found in their appearance on labour wards. And developments in technology like ultrasound have also increased fathers' access
to and involvement with infants even before birth (Sandelowski
1994:230-4).

The desire to move fathers from the periphery to centre stage in family relationships is certainly not sustained in the grand narratives of
developmental psychology. McKee and O'Brien (1982:11) say that the
centrality of "attachment" theory and its focus on the mother-infant
bond has meant that fathers' relationship to attachment has never been
fully investigated. Although mother-infant bonding still holds a hege-

monic position in narratives of developmental psychology and in the determination of the risk of child abuse, modern developmental psychologists like Rutter (1984:19) argue that children establish multiple attachments guided by their social situation. Research (cited by Rutter 1984:119) shows that a third of all single (as opposed to multiple) attachments are, in fact, to fathers, making "father absence" a much neglected area of investigation (Rutter 1984:50).

The insertion of a reconceptualized fatherhood into the North American family is only a partial response to fatherhood's marginality as an object of intellectual enterprise, and to the desire of some men to be more actively involved with their children. Active fatherhood has another political agenda. In Canada, as well as in the United States and in Britain, fatherhood has been identified as the "missing element in social policy" (Levine 1993:4). Levine suggests that it took the United States' "head start" program twenty-five years to "discover" the importance of paternal involvement. Head start families may be poor, but "tangential fathers" — boyfriends or male relatives — are in fact available in over 60% of families (Levine 1993:7). Fathers in this context are seen as important role models and not just as providers of material subsistence. Citing the United States Secretary of the Department of Health and Human Services, Levine (1993:5) concurs that "good" fathers play an indispensable role in the family and in the broader society.

This call for a male presence in the lives of children served by social policy agendas is also linked with the demand that fathers shoulder their material and financial responsibilities toward children. This demand has surfaced with a vengeance in the United States, in Britain, and also in Canada, where single mothers living on welfare have become the public enemies of the tax-paying citizen. It is the costs which missing fathers impose on welfare and Medicaid budgets which led the United States Secretary of the Department of Health and Human Services to claim that missing fathers were the social policy challenge of the era (Levine 1993:5). The Ontario government's (1995) savage cuts in welfare cheques have had an enormous impact on single mothers caught in the welfare trap. The explicit intention of these cuts is to encourage mothers to seek work even in very poorly paid jobs, or to pursue fathers for child support. The prospects of mothers finding work are further reduced by Ontario's cuts in licensed day-care places for school-aged children (Valpy, 1996). Much of the pressure for the reinsertion of the father into the North American (and British) family has occurred around a right-wing bid to shift the responsibility for welfare from the state and onto fathers.

What is Fatherhood Sociologically?

Fatherhood is a more flexible and ambiguous social role than motherhood in that it is less closely defined and monitored. It also contains an opt-out clause taken by the large number of fathers who lose track of their children within two years of separation. There is, for example, an alarming failure of non-custodial parents, most of whom are fathers, to pay child support. In Quebec, fewer than half of the 113,000 fathers ordered by the courts to pay child support do so either fully or on time. Twenty-five per cent of fathers pay nothing, opting out completely; thirty per cent pay only after being pressured by a collection agency. To deal with this situation, the governing Parti Québécois is bringing in Bill 60, legislation which invokes a direct debit system from paycheques, a system already in place in Ontario, New Brunswick, and Manitoba. Its aim is less to enforce a minimal conception of fathering, than to save $9 million in welfare payments to single mothers (*Montreal Gazette*, 26 May 1995:B2).

Fatherhood, like motherhood, has a plurality of styles and meanings construed around it. These meanings are organized by the specific social contexts in which fatherhood operates, negotiated by men themselves around the available array of masculinities. Fatherhood, again like motherhood, is constantly invented and reinvented by those who live as fathers. It is also organized by the networks of agencies supervising motherhood in the name of childhood. And it is organized by the legal codes and social policy frameworks in which it operates around issues of divorce and custody (McKee & O'Brien 1982:12-13, Lamb 1983:9). Fatherhood is positioned between the growing rates of labour force participation by mothers of young children, and the outcry against welfare mothers.

Fatherhood, like masculinity, is about the conditions of its acquisition. Different versions of fatherhood operate in different contexts, but in this book I am most concerned with versions of fatherhood invoked and invented in narratives concerning child abuse: with the administration of fatherhood and the meaning which fatherhood acquires in these processes.

Child Abuse and Fatherhood: an overview

The accusation made by the proponents of active fatherhood is that fatherhood is predominantly conceptualized as an object of social reform (McAdoo 1988:256-69). Jackson contends that social analyses provide a cast of "deviant fathers, dead fathers, fathers in prison, lonely fathers, absent fathers or mad fathers" (Jackson 1984:9).

This is to some extent sustained in narratives around child abuse. Court decisions and child protection interventions are often linked with treatment programs for alcoholism and drug abuse, and with attendance at therapy sessions for sexual offenders or self-help groups for "men who batter." For example, Cohen and Mannarino (1991:171-86), psychiatrists working at the University of Pittsburgh, document an incest case where the child protection workers refused to return two daughters to the home until the abusing father was removed. Front-line child protection workers in this kind of case are often involved in negotiations involving the police over whether it is advisable to press charges, and whether the father will co-operate in seeking therapy and in subsequently refraining from sexually predatory behaviour with children. Treatment and various kinds of legal sanction are, of course, the main strategies for dealing with abusive fathers.

Fathers are objects of intervention around attempts to reform specific kinds of behaviour. David Currie (1988), a social worker at the Forensic Service at the Clarke Institute of Psychiatry in Toronto, sets out a program of intervention to reform the behaviour of abusive men. Fathers are also punished for their behaviour in the judicial system, but the ways in which fathers are dealt with is both limited and rather heavy-handed. The difference between fathers and mothers is that mothers are more broadly seen as targets for family intervention.

Mothers feature in attempts, in perinatal medicine for example, to develop "good" mothering habits from the start. The approach with fathers, on the other hand, is to deal with specific pieces of problematic behaviour after the fact. Mothers are guardians of standards of family conduct, also charged with the responsibility for managing problematic fathering, as we saw in the last chapter. But fathers are more narrowly conceptualized as problematic and have to be "contained" and "managed" in order to limit their negative impact on family life. As long as they do not actually cause active harm, fathers do not come to the attention of child protection agencies.

The narratives reviewed in the chapter on motherhood provided a number of categories of problematic motherhood: high-risk motherhood, psychologically maladapted motherhood, negligent motherhood, devious motherhood, and dangerous motherhood. The range of problematic forms of fathering is more limited, however. The same professional narratives provide us with marginal and absent fathers, sexually dysfunctional fathers, and dangerous fathers. Fathers are a more limited object of family intervention, management and reform than mothers and this is consistent with the socially sanctioned primary responsibility of women for family matters. Popular culture and professional narratives are closely aligned in this respect.

Marginal and absent fatherhood

Marginality and absence have a number of resonances in child abuse narratives. Fathers are marginal and absent in the narratives themselves — distanced by the centrality and presence of mothers. Their marginality and absence are most evident in the two sites on which motherhood is construed as an indicator of risk and a target for social reform: perinatal medicine and public health strategies. Fathers barely appear as background noise in the Toronto community interventions run from the Public Health Department (Parents Helping Parents, Healthiest Babies Possible and the Healthy Beginnings Project). They are not seen as a viable target in reforming risky parenthood (in this context parenthood really does mean motherhood), although they are sometimes seen as a target for "treatment." But more on this later.

The window onto the family claimed by perinatal medicine in its quest to predict the risk of dangerousness affords fathers a particularly tangential relationship to the family. They scarcely appear in Ledger and Williams' (1981) "profile of high-risk families chart," taken from Gray (see Figure 1 on page 132-3). This chart pays no attention to the quality of the father's interaction with his infant, focusing instead on the father's relationship with the mother. Warning signs for hospital staff are seen to be hostile interaction between the parents, including chronic marital discord displayed in the labour and delivery period. Gray *et al.* (1976), using Helfer and Kempe's classic United States checklist for perinatal risk factors, concur with Ledger and Williams:

> Since the mother and baby are a "captive audience" during their postpartum confinement, a valuable opportunity is available to assess the family's support system at a time when it should be in operation. The most important aspect is the father's relationship to the mother and baby; how he begins to assume his new role, and how he supports his wife in assuming her new role. (Gray *et al.* 1976:386)[7]

Ledger and Williams' work with the British Columbia Ministry of Health mentions fathers in passing as a part of the maternal support system, but does not include the father's feelings about the new child in the calculation of risk:

> Does the mother have a spouse or "significant other?" Is the mother satisfied with spouse/male relationship?...
> What degree of support is offered by
> > Spouse/mate
> > Other children
> > Extended family
> > Friends...
> High Risk Warning Indicators (include)
> > No spouse, mate or significant other
> > Express dissatisfaction with spouse/mate relationship
> > Chronic marital discord, especially if focus of conflict

is around child bearing or child rearing... (Ledger
and Williams 1981:99)

In this construction of fatherhood, the father has only an indirect relationship to the family. His behaviour is conceptualized as having a bearing on the quality of mothering which can be offered in the family. But it is mothering and not fathering which is seen as significant. For perinatal medicine the quality of the father's relationship with the new baby is not particularly significant. The dominant social role of the man is that of a husband rather than a father; what counts is the quality of his relationship with the mother and the impact of *this* on her bonding with the infant. The father, then, has only a mediated relationship (through the mother) with the new infant. This certainly challenges the claims made on behalf of the "new-man-as-father" thesis which demands a more active role for fathers. And although this medicalized and highly restricted model in which fathers have relationships with mothers rather than their new infants does not necessarily prevail in the practices and research of other professionals, its influence lies in its function as part of an "early warning system" in which some families rather than others are brought to the attention of child protection workers.

Fathers are also seen as significant in organizing the social and financial, as well as the emotional, circumstances of a family. This is the second dimension to the marginality of fatherhood in perinatal medicine. The absence of a father or father figure is seen as an indicator of family stress and danger, alerting medical staff to the potential for family poverty and isolation. Ledger and Williams (1981) note this and so, much later, does Seagull (1987:43), who reports that over 29 per cent of physical abuse cases occurred in homes without a father or father substitute. This, too, indicates the marginal and mediated position which fathers occupy in the family as well as the extent to which mothers are implicated in physical abuse. Fathers are held responsible for levels of material provision which affect the mother's ability to manage the more direct business of emotional relationships within the family, the most significant of which is seen as her relationship with the baby. Whether emotional or financial, the father's role is that of a supporter and not a player in the central business of family life. But there is also one other piece of evidence for fathers as supporters, hinted at in Seagull's (1987:43) review of research findings based in the United States and in Britain: the high levels of physical abuse in homes without a father-figure. At least in the context of these studies, the father also operates as some form of protection, augmenting the dangerous effects of unsupported mothers on the family. There is, however, a debate in psychology about whether abuse is more or less likely to be found in single-parent households, most of which are headed by women. The roles of fathers, at least in perinatal medicine, are the most socially conservative possible. As the providers of material and emotional support to mothers they are "normally" expected to play only a marginal part in the family. The father in the abusing family fails to fulfil this marginal responsibility and so gives professional cause for concern.

This theme of absence and marginality is also found in personal narratives and memories of family life. The financial and material responsibilities of fathers and the difficulty of maintaining these are acknowledged by an African-American father speaking about the tenuousness of (black) family life in the United States.

> The men don't have jobs. The woman, she starts nagging. He don't have the money so he leaves. She ADC's it. If he had a job the family unit could come back together. Marriages break up because boys lose jobs, and some won't bring their money home.... The main cause [of family disintegration] is finance. (Rainwater 1970:169)

Betsy Petersen's (1991) memories of the father who sexually abused her are located at the other end of the class spectrum (the white, Canadian middle class), but also speak to the theme of father absence. In this case the danger is posed not by an absent father but by a father who is present and whose needs are given a central place in family life:

> So many of my memories are of my father as a doctor. Even his legendary sloppiness at home — the area around his armchair

was a wasteland of cigar ashes, socks and piled-up surgery jour-
nals — was seen in the family as something that went with being
a doctor. When he cooked he washed his hands a lot.... Surgeons
wash their hands a lot, my mother said, and he was used to having the nurses pick up after him in the operating room.

My father was gone a lot, taking care of his patients and going
to meetings: hospital staff meetings, two surgical societies, the
county medical society. Once he gave a talk on the radio: I
remember his voice booming out of the big console in the living
room while the dog barked madly. (Petersen 1991:14)

The father in the second extract, the doctor, is the least likely to be
"picked up" by the perinatal monitoring system; indeed, he is more
likely to be a part of that monitoring system. This is, perhaps, the
major failing of perinatal medicine's rendering of the family: as well as
seeing fathers in the most minimal sense possible, it is highly class-
selective in its scrutiny.

Sexually dysfunctional fatherhood

The sexually dysfunctional father — the classic child sex abuser — is
primarily the construction of psychology. He is rather more dangerous
than the absent or disruptively marginal father of perinatal medicine,
who is simply seen as adding tensions and stresses to the mother-infant
bonding process. Although sexually predatory behaviour has a place in
the cultures of normal, even hegemonic, masculinity, its expression
within the family does not. Consideration of sexual abuse by psychology, in fact, privileges incest over other forms of sexual abuse. Within
these psychological studies the focus is also on the characteristics of
mothers who "fail to protect" rather than on father perpetrators
(Strand 1991:378).

When the sexually dysfunctional father is discussed he is conceptualized as a collection of socio- and psychopathologies, although these
are not as well developed as the psychopathology of motherhood.
Dawson's (1982) review of literature and research developed as a train-

ing program for the Ontario Ministry of Community and Social Services suggests that in incest cases the sexually dysfunctional father is dominant and controlling within families where the sexual unavailability of the mother combines with the daughter's adolescence. The father's sexual dysfunction consists of a fixated and arrested psychosexual development in which he "regresses" to an earlier, conflict-free stage of development to overcome his feelings of "inadequacy and incompetence." According to this schema the sexually dysfunctional father may also be an "introvert," a rationalizer," a "tyrant" or an "alcoholic." Bentovim *et al.*'s (1988) British psychoanalytic account of child sexual abuse offers two pathological "types" of father in the "regressed offender" and the "fixated offender."

> Fixated offenders are those individuals who have emerged from their own childhood with a sexual orientation toward children. Regressed offenders are those individuals who may have reached an adequate sexual relationship with an adult, but in the presence of particular crises, for example, the illness or death of a partner, find themselves turning towards a child sexually. (Bentovim *et al.* 1988:32)

These authors go on to say that this neat distinction is not particularly helpful in practice, as the same kind of childhood can produce both "types." In Canada, Bagley (1985:68), while not using the psychoanalytic concepts of sexual dysfunction, regressed or fixated, nevertheless holds that sexual abusers are a "type" in psychological and personality terms. Bagley points out that "powerless males" with "inadequate personalities" use children for sex.

> Adults who sexually assault children, including their own, are frequently described as inadequate personalities who have created or experienced disordered marital relationships and who often abuse alcohol. These clinical profiles do not contradict the argument that child sexual assault is caused, fundamentally, by a basic value principle which underpins the exploitation of all children. The argument asserts that weak and relatively powerless males use

children (usually, but not always, female children) not only for [175] sexual gratification, but for the exercise of power and status as well. (Bagley 1985:68)

The nature of the sexual dysfunctions and psychopathologies of the sexually dysfunctional father, however, is not in itself significant. The context in which it becomes significant is the family containing a passive mother who "allows" her children to be abused, referred to in Chapter Four. Fatherhood pathologies and sexual dysfunctions, then, are not inherently problematic; they are only contextually so, because fathers in child protection terms also have a relationship to their families which is significantly mediated by mothers. It is thus the breakdown of important forms of mediation in the family which is problematic, and not sexually predatory behaviour itself. Sawula's (1989) risk assessment guide for sexual abuse to be used by child protection workers highlights, in considering family dynamics overall, the "Ability of Non-Offending Parent to Protect" as a significant factor in risk.

The focus on psychological factors in locating sexually predatory or violent fathers is a controversial one. Currie's (1988) treatment approach to "The Abusive Husband" stresses that it is social context and not individual psychology which is the problem. Male anger, he says, is not the cause of family violence; men get angry in many situations, yet they only vent this anger in the context of their families because it is socially acceptable to do so. In this argument the overall cultural context and the social structures which condone intra-family violence are seen as the issue and not individual personalities. A similar focus on culture and social structure rather than psychology is found in the Report of the Special Advisor to the Minister of National Health and Welfare on Child Abuse in Canada (1990), which, despite its alarming estimates of child sexual abuse implicating men as predators, blames patriarchy (as a socially sanctioned system of male power), and not sexually dysfunctional men, for abuse. Wash and Knudson-Martin's (1994) account of incestuous fathers in the *Journal of Contemporary Family Therapy* report from interviews with sexually abusive fathers that incest has more to do with conceptions of masculinity which stress entitlement than with defective personalities:

The entitlement is connected to perceptions of both masculinity and family relationships. Incest occurred in the context of a building-up of failure in these areas and conflicts regarding intimacy needs and needs to be in control. (Wash and Knudson-Martin 1994:398)

So not for the first time in looking at the rendering of the family by professional narratives do we see a tension between locating problems in the individual and locating them in the overall social structures in which individuals operate.

Managing Intimacy

Professional narratives on child abuse rarely address the issue of managing intimate relationships between fathers and children. The exception to this are some of the professional narratives developed around family therapy. This is not surprising, since this is the arena in which individuals are most likely to confess their feelings about the boundaries of family intimacy. According to Wash and Knudson-Martin (1994:402-3) there is a conflict among incestuous fathers between the need for control and the need for intimacy:

The helplessness felt in response to needing others was problematic. Inevitably their tactics for staying in control would interfere with their ability to be close.... He [referring to one of their informant/patients] did not like his anger, because it made him feel "soft" and "out of control." Sex, he said "puts me back in control" ... "I don't try to get close ... if I'm sexual I'll be close to them"...

In this father's case sex is a substitute for intimacy with children. Otherwise there is a marked divergence between professional and personal narratives over the issue of how the boundaries of intimacy are managed within families, and where intimacy becomes either inappropriate or sexually abusive. The difficulties posed by these boundaries and the management of desire within the family are, however, raised in

personal narratives. Some of the questions raised around the boundaries of family sexuality are revealed in a stepfather's confession about
his feelings for his stepdaughter, made in the context of Hite's research
on the family:

> My stepdaughter, I raised her from the age of four. I loved that lit-
> tle girl (still do, only she's not little) and, because her mother was
> out of town, would have tampax-trained if it came to that, but
> she trusted me, and she still does. I don't see her much because
> she lives far away, but we get along very well. There is a sexual
> attraction; I know it and so does she. I wouldn't hurt that girl for
> the whole universe, because she trusts me not to! She's going to be
> a helluva woman! Sexual activity can take a back-seat in this one.
> Would I go to bed with her if I could? I'll be damned if I know!
> But I would still like to comb her hair, sooth her bee stings, bathe
> her, and have her asleep in my lap! (Hite 1994:222)

The boundaries of tender caring and sexual contact for some fathers
(and those in the position of father) are more often difficult to define
and complex to negotiate than professional narratives acknowledge. In
Hite's survey most fathers' physical contact with their children reached
a cut-off point between five years old and adolescence as both sensed it
was no longer appropriate to have close physical contact. In the following extract a father discusses his enjoyment at the physical tending
of his sons without raising questions about the boundary between intimacy and sexuality. Here we have a sense of an empathic fathering
which is focused on child care rather than on more traditional male
responsibilities of work and discipline:

> One of my greatest joys was sitting in a chair or on a couch and
> holding them for hours as they slept. This way I could look at
> them, I could feel their soft cheeks, listen to their gentle breath-
> ing. Today I am their Superstar, their number one. I would take
> over night feedings whenever my wife was either too sick or too
> tired to do it. The love and affection I have for my children is deep
> and gratifying.... No matter how busy I am, I find time for my

family. Another job I can find tomorrow. Another family is impossible to find. (Hite 1994:325)

Dangerousness and Fatherhood

Constructions of fatherhood in terms of dangerousness dominate narratives on child abuse. Dangerousness, as indicated in the last chapter, is a gendered conception. Whereas mothers — with the exception of a small minority — are not "seen" as dangerous, fathers are. This gender dichotomy is, significantly, also sustained by dominant trends in the narratives of Canadian feminism, and by cultural scripts linking hegemonic masculinity with violence. The connection between fathers and violence is in part filtered through official government narratives which collapse different forms of abuse of women, children, elders, and other vulnerable groups as though they were part of an undifferentiated mass. Upon closer examination this mass of aggression has two significant dimensions: the first concerns the involvement of men in spousal abuse, and the second their involvement in child sexual abuse.

Spousal abuse is not one of the central issues of this book, but it has an important connection with child abuse in (professional and individual) narratives, and it plays a part in the construction of fatherhood as dangerous. Vale (1989) notes that a large number of North American studies have seen a correlation between child abuse and other forms of family violence, indicating that while spousal abuse and child abuse are distinct, they are often closely related.

> He [Murray Strauss's 1983 survey] found that 7%-19% of parents who reported no marital violence frequently abused their children. Fathers who assaulted their wives did not show an elevated scale of abusing children unless they assaulted their wives more than 3 times a year. 50% of these men frequently abused their children. Mothers who were assaulted by their spouses showed a consistently higher rate of abusing their children.... From these various incidence studies, it seems clear that child abuse and spousal abuse are distinct but often closely interrelated phenomena.(Vale 1989:3)

Most of the research literature on dangerousness is concerned with adult-to-adult violence. Currie's (1988) attempt to establish an intervention strategy with dangerous men is also directed specifically at spousal abuse. The British Columbia Task Force (1992), which firmly casts men and fathers in the role of perpetrators of family violence, is concerned mainly with domestic violence directed at women. It cites two of its expert witnesses to make this point:

> Men beat their wives because they are permitted to do so and nobody stops them, and women are beaten because they are trained and forced and maintained into dependence and nobody helps them....
>
> Violence has a male face. The greatest threat to women comes from the men they live with. (Report of the British Columbia Task Force on Family Violence 1992:73)

When this report moves on to discuss child abuse it shifts to sexual abuse in order to maintain the thesis of male dangerousness. But there is no evidence specifically linking fathers with physical abuse, even in its lethal forms; it is something for which fathers share equal responsibility with mothers. In looking at Rosenthal's analysis of the Colorado Central (child abuse) Registry, Vale (1989) makes the following point about physical abuse.

> In general, men are more likely than women (53.8%) to abuse boys, and women were more likely than men (52%) to abuse girls.... Some important inferences can be made from this data. Assuming that women are much more involved in child care than men, it is surprising that the incidence of male abusers is in the 50% range [for physical abuse]. Possibly men are more prone to abuse than women. Still, women are quite numerous as abusers. (Vale 1989:2)

Anecdotal evidence in personal narratives also implicates mothers and fathers equally as perpetrators of physical abuse. So there is no reason based on the evidence of involvement in physical abuse to pin-point fathers and father substitutes as being violent toward children.

The construction of fatherhood as dangerous in child abuse narratives, then, rests on their involvement with sexual abuse. As Bentovim *et al.* (1988) claim in their study of sexual abuse, "There is no explanation of why children are sexually abused. Over 90% of abusers are men, and a number of attempts have been made to try to explain this phenomenon" (Bentovim *et al.* 1988).

The Report of the Special Advisor to the Minister of National Health and Welfare (1990:13), also cited in earlier chapters, suggests that 95 per cent of sex abusers are male and the majority of victims female. This overwhelmingly implicates men, although not necessarily fathers. Although the report blames patriarchal social structures, the behaviour of individual men (and women) is the means by which these structures are performed, so it is not a question of individual agency or social structure. Individuals operate making decisions in social contexts. The report goes on to stress the gendered dimensions of dangerousness:

> There is a very clear gender dimension to child sexual abuse. In well over 90% of reported cases of sexual abuse, the offenders are men. When women are involved, it is often because they are forced to or encouraged to abuse by men. The Badgley Committee found that 98.8% of offenders were male and 1.2% were female. Our society continues to evolve from a value system that placed men in the dominant role and women and children in a subordinate role. (Report of the Special Advisor to the Minister of National Health and Welfare on Child Sexual Abuse in Canada 1990:17)

The particular association between fathers and dangerousness involved in sexual abuse, while clearly implicating men does not necessarily point to fathers or father substitutes, though father-daughter incest has received a great deal of attention in psychiatric and psychological research. Finkelhor's (1979) classic study of sex abuse establishes brothers and male cousins as a more significant group of perpetrators than fathers. And Kendall Tackett and Simon (1987:242) claim that sexual [181] abuse by father-figures is not necessarily more common, but is certainly more damaging than abuse by other men. It is therefore more likely to lead to clinical settings, which gives a distorted impression of the extent of father's involvement in the sexual abuse of children.

The central problem associated with dangerousness in terms of child protection intervention concerns verification and prediction. Indicators of sexual abuse dangerousness are often located, at least in psychiatry, in the man's psychological biography and include items such as a history of behaviour indicating sexual "deviation," a "history of drug or alcohol abuse," and "low self esteem" (Gardner 1987:7). Bentovim *et al.*'s (1988) report on the intake of abusing families reported by social workers also points to these more psycho-social factors in the profiles of sexual abusers:

> However, there are indications of high levels of alcohol abuse, the habitual use of violence, unemployment, the absence of the other adult, and considerable incidence of marital problems and sexual difficulties. (Bentovim *et al.* 1988:35)

If this list of the social and psychological features of abusers is an attempt to draw a profile to aid the prediction of dangerousness, then it is surprisingly vague and poorly established. This is particularly so given the centrality of dangerousness in strategies aimed at the prediction and management of child abuse. If dangerousness cannot be predicted with any great confidence or certainty then perhaps this psychological profiling of men has no basis or validity. In this context we might want to review the usefulness of constructing these categories of fathering pathology. Verification is a different issue, but constructing dangerousness around personality types is not the best means of verifying abuse either. The stories of children may be the best route to verification. The dangerousness thesis attached to masculinity and then extended to fatherhood lies less in any established connection between fathers and various forms of child abuse, than in a general cultural association of masculinity with violence and sexually predatory behaviour. At least some of the professional and government narratives concerned with family dangerousness rely on an association between masculinity and violence in their assumptions, in their research findings, and in their perceptions of family life.

That is not to imply that dangerousness in fathering is not a legitimate concern. It is, although it may not be as hegemonic and pervasive as some professional and official narratives suggest. Hearn's (1990) point about the violence embedded in "normal masculinity," however, is well taken. Stories of dangerous fathers also abound in the personal narratives of adult survivors. Here is the story of an adult woman survivor of sexual abuse describing her father:

> "What do you think, [he would say] you're better than others?" He was always demanding things and yelling. "Why is this house like this? Why isn't supper cooked?" I feared him, though we could talk. My brothers were never pushed to do anything. They were supposed to do dishes but they hid them and got away with it. My father beat me until I was 15. One time he called me a fucking whore. That really hurt me. (Hoff 1990:27)

In the following individual narrative, a young woman is writing a letter to her parents about her relationship with her abusive father. This clearly makes the point that it was the father who made home a dangerous place:

> Relations between Dad and myself have reached an end-point for me.... Dad and I have had extremely poor relations for a long time now, and I guess that can go on for years of unhappiness and tension.... But years of your terrible temper, Dad, and your unhappiness and frustration have worn away at not only you but also me. I really want no part of that any more. You try to efface other people constantly, and I resent you for that. You totally ignore the feelings of others, and that is too bad, because every situation in life doesn't hinge on you. It is constantly necessary to "escape" you to have peace of mind.... You treated me terribly and were cruel to me for years, although there was a time when things were good between us.... I was in fear of you and imprisoned until I left home for school... (Hite 1994:190-1)

The personal narratives in which men explain their relationship to violence and the part which violence plays in their lives are rather revealing. Here is a man speaking about male violence in the context of Hoff's (1993) study of abused women. This study is unusual in its more open approach to male violence — asking why men are violent rather than just documenting the effects of violence on the bodies and lives of women — and in its allowing men to speak for themselves.

> When I was a kid I hit my sisters and they hit me. When I was in third grade I hauled off and hit a girl who called me names.... I gave her a black eye. The school called my parents, but they did-n't say anything to me because I didn't say anything. I felt terrible socially to have hurt her.... What would people think? I know a lot of really gentle men who had violent fathers and were roughed up as kids. My life is a history of getting beaten up and not defending myself. (Hoff 1993:129)

Another man speaks in similar terms about what it was like to be a male child and how that impacts on the adult self.

> They've [non-violent men] always had additional information, availability of more choices. If you'd have known me before, you'd have probably called me a violent man. If you threatened me I'd have broken your arm. It all comes from fear — my reaction to threat and fear was violence. For example, there was a bat in my house.... I caught the bat and pulverized it, out of fear.... When I was a kid I knocked a nun down when she confronted me about my temper, and I kicked a priest in the shins. I fought my way through school. I used to be labelled angry and obnoxious. I was programmed. I had to be tough and that made me fearful. I was also a role, an angelic, an altar boy and president of my class but I could do no wrong. I was two roles. There was a kind and gen-tle me even then.... I helped old people. I loved my mother.... I don't have to be tough any more, because of the emergence of that part of me that is kind and gentle. (Hoff 1993:129-30)

Sometimes, too, violence is a means of showing a kind of affection, as some of the men in Wash and Knudson-Martin's (1994) study indicate in their personal narratives: "I loved my father very much... He would throw us across the room ... but it was a good family" (Wash and Knudson-Martin 1994:400).

Normal fatherhood

In practice "normal" fatherhood is enforced (minimally) in court decisions regarding custody and access to children, and in the enforcement of child support payments. It is enforced in the supervisory activities of front-line child protection workers directed at a father's behaviour within the family. It is enforced in agreements with child protection workers regarding "treatment" and forms of therapy as conditions of access to family life for fathers. The boundaries of fatherhood are maintained by the actions of therapists, child protection workers, psychiatrists, and psychologists, and by legal instruments. In this way the boundaries of fatherhood resemble those of motherhood, although the activities which take place within these boundaries are quite differently conceptualized.

There is no explicit narrative on "normal fatherhood" in texts concerned with child abuse. Normal fatherhood has to be winnowed out of the meanings construed around fatherhood as marginal and absent, sexually dysfunctional, and dangerous already reviewed. As with motherhood, it was the need to administer problematic fatherhood which created an implicit narrative on normality. The normal father in the narratives of perinatal medicine, for example, operates as significant background social and financial support to the family, leaving child-rearing and the emotional business of family life to the mother. The normal father of perinatal medicine is hence tangential to the main relationships making up the family; he has only a mediated relationship to his family through his relationship to the mother. The normal father in the constructions of psychopathology which make up sexual dysfunction has a sexual relationship with his wife and not with his children. The normal father, by implication, does not have problems

with self-esteem or abuse alcohol. He does not have a history of sexual deviation or other psycho-sexual pathologies.

In short, the normal father has a very sketchy and negative appearance in professional narratives, from which it is hard to imagine what positive qualities and advantages he brings to the job. The normal father in many agency narratives belongs to another era from the "new man as active father." The normal father is clearly organized around the 1950s functionalist model of Parsonian sociology, where he serves as background financial and emotional support to the mother, who is the key broker in day-to-day family business and in emotional relationships. But the normal father of child abuse narratives is even a shadow of the Parsonian model, which has many positive, albeit gender-specific qualities. Even Winnicott (1991:17-18), the famous psychotherapist writing in the 1950s who embraced the Parsonian mother-centred invention of the family viewed fathers as an "add-on" part of the family, but one which enriches children's lives significantly. He says:

> if the father is there and wants to get to know his own child the child is fortunate, and in the happiest circumstances father vastly enriches his child's world... (Winnicott 1991:116)

The sketchy portrait of fatherhood in professional narratives is, of course, the result of a particular window onto the family. Accounts of fatherhood in family therapy situations are fuller and more complex, grounded as they are in the richness and detail of everyday lives. Personal narratives also present a more vivid and rounded portrait of fatherhood. Professional narrative constructions, on the other hand, are necessarily flattened caricatures — versions of fatherhood which render it amenable to agency intervention. When fatherhood is administered it takes on a particular appearance.

Fatherhood is rendered in terms of simple pathologies so that it can be a target for social management. There is little point to describing child abuse and a great deal of point in taking action to deal with it. If family dangerousness is a major problem because of its effect on children, and fathers are overwhelmingly associated with dangerousness, then there is a case to be made for developing strategies aimed directly at reducing the dangers posed by the behaviour of fathers. There are interventions which aim at reconstructing abusing fathers, but it is not clear how widespread or effective they are. Indeed, there are some forms of "treatment" available to sex offenders: Giaretto (1982:276), for example, stresses the importance of fathers being treated in father-daughter incest cases. Part of this treatment involves the father admitting guilt and taking responsibility for the abuse. This is, however, hindered by the adversarial system of the law which mitigates against the admission of guilt.

This reminds us that treatment programs are often linked with correctional services. Punishment and criminalization are the dominant, although questionably the most effective, method used to deal with dangerous fathers who are more readily criminalized than treated. Currie's (1988:1-6) "how-to" manual approach to "anger management" is a direct attempt to deal with men, but as violent spouses and not as violent fathers. Similarly, Wolfe's (1990) small-scale longitudinal pilot study in London, Ontario, which offers adolescent boys who are potentially Crown wards strategies in personal conduct other than aggression, is also a direct attempt to deal with male behaviour. The aim of Wolfe's project is to follow up to see if intervention affects the ways in which the boys conduct themselves when they become fathers. Others take a broader view, asserting the need for social change. Cohn, Finkelhor and Holmes (1985:9) argue for a reconstruction of fatherhood, calling for "more flexible male roles" which challenge the social exemption of men from child rearing, something which they see as a cause of abuse: "In a society that encourages predatory male sexuality, male aggressivity and male irresponsibility towards children, [they claim], it will be hard to prevent sexual abuse."

Concluding Comments on the Gendered Organization of Child-Abuse Narratives

There are some important differences, clearly organized by gender, in the inventions of motherhood and fatherhood which occur around child abuse. Fathers are perpetrators of abuse and sometimes second-generation victims.[8] Mothers are overwhelmingly victims, and rarely perpetrators; their interactions with children and their psycho-social profiles are taken as indicators of abuse. Fathers' behaviour is also seen as an indicator of abuse, although it is conceptualized in more restricted terms. They are expected to have only an indirect connection with family business which is centrally mediated by mothers. Both mothers and fathers are the object of psychological investigation and personality assessment for abusive traits, and are also major targets of different kinds of social management strategies. While mothers are predominantly held only indirectly responsible for child abuse, they have a more direct responsibility for managing the effects of abusive fathers on the family. And while fathers are held more directly responsible for abuse, they have a lesser responsibility for the social management of family relationships. Some of the key cultural assumptions about the differences between men and women are inscribed in these professional narratives. These differences, however, appear in particular forms. They are filtered by the professional knowledge systems and agency practices through which the family is administered. Attention to the family for reasons of child abuse crucially transforms the family while holding it roughly in line with broader cultural and social trends.

Notes

1. "... to read all the central literature on fatherhood — given a first class university archive and a plentiful supply of coffee and notepaper — should take about thirty-six working hours" (Jackson 1984:9)

2. David Morgan (1992) borrows this concept from Robert Connell (1987) and develops it.

3. The concept of hegemonic masculinity does not really offer an explanation of why and how some versions of masculinity are more

embedded in social practices and gendered encounters than others without recourse to general observations about the cultural privileging of one set of images over another.

4. This side-steps arguments developed in sociobiology about the natural/historical association between men and war-like activities used to demonstrate that violence is an inherent part of a man's nature.

5. A third option is a traditional, clinical one which does not conflate violence quite so much with gender but differentiates "violent" from "normal" behaviour.

6. African-American fathers are traditionally portrayed as abandoning their family responsibilities. As *American Demographics* (August 1993:23) points out, this is not accurate as Black and Hispanic married fathers are just as involved with their children as are white married fathers. Rainwater and Atherton's (1970) *Behind the Ghetto Walls: Black Families in a Federal Slum* provides some moving first-person narratives discussing family relationships.

7. The classic studies of Helfer and Kempe developed in Denver provide the model for this. These studies were used by Gray, who worked with Helfer and Kempe, and by Ledger and Williams, who worked with the British Columbia Ministry of Health. In this way the United States' quest for the pathological family enters Canadian medicine. Note also here the ranking of mother followed by the baby. This is highly significant.

8. Compared to those of women there are few published and popularly available personal accounts of fatherhood. This is in part because of differences in "invitations to speak" and reasons to tell a personal story. It is not that women have monopolized the art of personal confession, but that public attention given to child abuse has favoured the memories and reminiscences of women who are able to present themselves as abuse victims. Men are predominantly seen as perpetrators and as such the invitations to them to speak are more limited to their roles as "survivors." For some of these reasons there are few first-person accounts of fatherhood; the stories cited here are largely *about* rather than *by* fathers.

CONCLUSIONS

THE family is usefully conceptualized in sociology as a narrative enterprise: it is generated, or *talked-up*, through the many ways in which it is "dealt" with in social policy, and in fiscal and political arenas. The family is generated in the minutiae of the daily performance of family in the lives of its members: actions and interactions are also (unwritten) narratives. It is a narrative production with multiple meanings generated through definite social apparatuses. Conceptualizing the family as generated and sustained through narratives means that we can think about the family in terms which are neither overly abstract, nor simply descriptions of living arrangements. It means we can think about some of the ways in which families are produced and sustained. It means we can see the family as a dynamic set of arrangements which are always being renegotiated. The family, then, is an infinitely varied set of representations in which individuals enter into dialogues with each other and with the administrative apparatuses through which they are (powerfully) dealt with.

The family as a living arrangement — and as an object of sociological enquiry — is both administratively and existentially generated. In this book I have argued that the administrative and the existential enter into a dialogical relationship with each other. Social and administrative categories shape lives, and lives give shape and meaning to administrative categories. It is through these dialogical processes of negotiation that subjectivities, identities, and conceptions of the self are formed and transformed. The family is hence a site of multiple meaning on which the constitution of subjects takes place. The exercise of power as a set of social relationships does not occur solely through the administration of the family (as Foucault and Donzelot suggest), but in the dialogues between the administrative and the existential. The power to name and classify, through agency management strategies, and, most powerfully of all, self-regulation, produces families which are all inevitably hybrids. Theoretically, then, the family is neither the object of social regulation (as Foucault and Donzelot suggest) nor a domain of free will and individual choice. It is precisely created at the boundaries between the individual and an extensive (but selective) regulatory apparatus.

I have argued that the family is described in particular ways in its encounter with child abuse, formed and transformed in particular ways in the administrative and existential dialogues which occur around such abuse. I have not argued that this is an unwarranted intrusion on private affairs; rather, I have been concerned to describe the impact on the family of its encounter with child abuse, and the kinds of social relationships and family "positions" which are created in this encounter. My narrative is not intended as a critique of social regulation; social regulation which protects the rights of children is entirely justified. Child abuse is a serious, persistent and seemingly insoluble social and individual problem. An effective child protection apparatus is essential to any society which upholds notions of social justice and human equality and which applies these concerns to children. Childhood is personhood in process, but defending the rights of children not to be beaten, neglected and violated requires an apparatus which poses all sorts of practical, philosophical and moral difficulties. Child abuse is difficult to see and uncomfortable to believe in, deeply embedded in the performance of family life and the myths surrounding it. It raises some fundamental questions about the nature of the family itself as well as the administrative invention of the family as a problem to be dealt with by social agencies. These questions concern the boundaries of adult-child relationships, styles of parenting, and the management of intimacy.

Throughout this book I have described some of the ways in which the family is conceptualized, spoken about, and acted upon by the agencies on whom the responsibility for dealing with abuse devolves. I have suggested that in its association with child abuse the family is rendered in administrative terms. The social and family roles of mother, father and child which have fragmented, varied and lived dimensions in individual narratives and recollections of family life become flattened and held static when the family is administered as a social problem. This administrative rendering of the family is entirely understandable:

it makes the family "actionable." And it is here that the complexity of the family is actually confessed. Complexity may be amenable to sociological description, but when it comes to *dealing* with child abuse the family is not being *defined*: it is being *acted upon*. It has to be positioned so that practitioners can do what they have to do with it — change it or manage it — so as to protect children.

The administration of the family occurs through a number of filters. The first is a set of background assumptions — implicit knowledge about what the family is — derived from sociology, psychology, psychotherapy, and so on. The second set of filters concerns the professional obligations of the agencies involved in the management of child abuse. Some of these obligations are prescribed by child protection laws, and reflect the division of professional competence between professionals working with child abuse. The third reflects the professional practices of the agencies concerned: some offer healing and therapy, some the active management of daily family affairs, and some are charged with providing evidence of abuse. It is through these filters that the family is positioned as something which can be acted upon. Frontline child protection agencies, therapists, judges, the police, psychologists, and physicians are confronted with child abuse's narratives of human misery on a daily basis. These professionals make difficult decisions with far-reaching implications for people's lives. So in order for them to be able to make these decisions they must administratively reinvent the lives of the families with which they deal: complex, dynamic, and intimate human interactions become entrenched personality "types" pursuing predictable scripts; moments of pathology become a way of life which must be apprehended and dealt with. These are not purely administrative impositions; they are ways of "seeing" families with which all families enter into a dialogue as active human agents making decisions, albeit in admittedly highly circumscribed circumstances. These are dialogues in which the boundaries of family conduct are negotiated with those charged with the supervision of childhood.

The active management of family life comes with the social demand to protect children — it is inseparable from it. In order to protect children, distressed individuals have to be turned into social categories. This is not in question. The problem is not that families are rendered an object of social management; indeed, certain members of families may welcome the management of their affairs — adolescents who need to challenge their parents, for example, or women who feel trapped by violent or abusive men. The problem is rather the terms in which the family is rendered as an object of social management. Some of these terms are highly problematic, as I have pointed out. They have social implications and affect the ways in which we see and think about both the family and child abuse. The boundary around dangerousness and normality, as I have argued, is organized by race, gender and class distinctions: distinctions which child abuse has helped to generate and develop.

One of the most serious outcomes of the ways in which the family is rendered an object of administrative intervention is the problematization of the poor — in any case the most over-administered and highly problematized part of any society. Child abuse adds to the list of reasons — street danger, crime, drug abuse, prostitution, and multiple forms of delinquency — why the poor are a target for social management strategies. And the entanglement of child abuse with the general management of an "underclass" is something which should be subjected to serious scrutiny for three reasons. First, this is an unjust over-burdening of a population which lives in the most difficult of social circumstances. Second, there is no demonstrated over-representation of the poor among those who abuse children. This is especially the case if we consider that the poor are already overscrutinized. Third, this is not the most effective way to provide child protection. If children are to be effectively protected then the practices of all families, and not just the poor, should be open to question. Professionals should not be put off inquiring into the affairs of those who have the social competence to represent themselves in terms of "good" child care and who live in an "ordered" domestic domain. Breaking the class-child abuse association may also allow us to think more broadly about child abuse. What about its more subtle forms — the emotional pressure to succeed, the humiliation and excessive regulation practised by socially "successful" parents as ways of dealing with their children? Instead, child abuse has provided an opportunity to interrogate and manage the family affairs of the poor and socially disadvantaged.

An equally serious outcome of the ways in which child abuse has administered the family is the consignment of mothers and fathers to extremely traditional roles organized by stereotypical notions of masculinity and femininity which have otherwise long since faded in prominence. In medicine and psychology in particular some of the most rigid notions of family are forged around the quest to identify family pathology. I have argued that motherhood is a pivotal role in the detection and social management of abuse, not least because of the central part played by mothers in servicing particular conceptions of childhood. Notions of the normal and the pathological invoked in staking out forms of motherhood offer ample opportunity for self-censorship. The construction of the bad mother operates as a warning to all mothers, and when self-censorship fails there are some fairly Draconian management strategies offered by those with expertise in childhood. Women need to reconsider their own relationship to child abuse in broader terms. The dominant attachment to a victim-status means that women permanently retain a speaking-position rooted in their own memories of childhood. "Growing-up" may involve switching to the position of perpetrator and examining more honestly mothers' relationship to violence in child-rearing. But only in making this move can mothers critically examine and support each other's child-rearing practices. Clearly we need more flexible and modern conceptions of the family which are in line with the ways in which people live. Fathers need to be taken more seriously as central family members with more extensive responsibilities toward children. We need to think about more effective ways than through the penal system for dealing with abusing fathers. The family needs to be rendered an object of social management in terms which are not class-, gender-, and age-discriminatory, and should reflect the flexibility in practical mothering and fathering arrangements which families negotiate with all of the complexity of relationships and residence patterns this brings.

Administrative renderings of the family have some more general social outcomes which go well beyond the families being administered. First, there is an interplay between professional conceptions of the family and (hegemonic) popular conceptions of family. The mapping of subjectivities in terms of class- and gender- specific categories of pathology — negligent mothers, dangerous fathers, and so on — enter popular conceptions of child abuse. Some, though not all, of these pathologies have become popularized as ways of seeing and explaining child abuse. Most seductive are the popular conceptions that fathers are dangerous and sexually predatory, that mothers are passive victims, and that children are either evil or innocent. Some administrative terms enter popular narratives more easily than others because they find support there. For example, the casting of masculinity in terms of dangerousness occurs in other domains and other administrative narratives so that an association is already established. Hence professionals often help to define the terms in which a social problem may be seen more generally, as well as dealt with professionally.

Second, categories construed in professional narratives are absorbed into the ways in which people think about themselves. People who are categorized as socially problematic enter into a dialogue with the professional categories through which they are positioned. We saw at several points throughout this book examples of individual narratives having absorbed or otherwise responded to professional explanations of the "problem." The stories told by professionals impinge on the stories which people tell about their own lives. Administrative categories and identities enter into the ways in which people think about and explain themselves and their lives. It is not that individuals simply "take on" professional explanations of who they are; individuals also contest and manipulate professional narratives. But in either case they are forced to take such narratives into account.

Rendering the family an object of administrative action in terms which are more flexible and in line with lived family relationships, and which respect some basic tenets of social justice, requires a reconsideration of the professional narratives through which the family is generated. Social agencies may be able to rethink the terms in which they deal with families by emphasizing lived family forms and notions of social justice in the practical details of their work. Requiring social agencies to consider carefully and critically the social outcomes of their administrative renderings would be a starting-point. But there is another way of approaching this. Are all these categories of pathology and implicit normality essential for the management of abusive family life?

Are there more effective ways of thinking about the family which bet- [195] ter protect children and which support and respect the integrity of dis- tressed parents? Administrative renderings of the family are very pow- erful and should be used sparingly. There is really no justification for generating an administrative category which does not facilitate effec- tive intervention. Do the psychologists' "maps" to pathology, for exam- ple, actually effect changes in family behaviour which lessen danger- ousness or which help people deal with their internal anguish? Only the administrative constructions of the family which have a practical bene- fit are really justified. Child abuse, because of its importance as a social issue, has generated professional inflation — it is everywhere and everything is connected with it. This is an understandable professional reaction given the gravity of the issue, but it has some unhelpful side- effects in how the family is seen and understood. The family is crucial- ly shaped in its encounter with child abuse, but we must be careful not to over-shape it, prescribing standards of normality and documenting pathologies which have no practical outcome in terms of child safety.

The least constructive and overly prescriptive aspects of the family as an administrative invention concern prediction. Perhaps the time has come to admit that child abuse is not predictable and to concentrate instead on dealing effectively with its occurrence or suspected occur- rence. Attempts at prevention should be confined to broader social ini- tiatives affecting communities as a whole, such as daycare provision ini- tiatives which unburden the family, and should not be about identifying pathological families and individuals. Concentrating professional expertise on managing abusing families and helping them to reconfig- ure their relationships certainly would be more helpful than prediction.

Abandoning the role of prediction, agencies must look more closely at what professional expertise they have to offer. While psychology and psychiatry have an obvious therapeutic role to play in healing and reconstructing family relationships, those in the medical professions should seriously reconsider what expertise they are able to provide that makes an effective contribution to the management of child abuse. Although medicine has an important role to play in verification, it should look critically at the social contexts in which its medical judge- ments are made, because these are often quite discriminatory.

Psychologists should be careful about labelling what they are not willing or able to treat. But it is child protection workers who have the most continuous relationships with abusing families. This places them in a good position to develop their own field of specific expertise rather than relying on the related but more removed expertise of other professionals. Agencies, in other words, should specialize more rather than attempt a narrative convergence or excessive inter-agency co-operation. They should specialize precisely in those practical solutions that they can professionally apply to the problem. Along with this narrower professional perspective agencies also need a broader, more political and critical perspective which is capable of recognizing the power and broader impact of professional judgement on the construction of social forms. Sociology, along with psychoanalysis, psychology, social policy, anthropology, and cultural studies are disciplines which have an important intellectual and critical contribution to make in conceptualizing the family as a complex and flexible set of forms which are construed in narrative.

REFERENCES

Adamakos, Harry, Kathleen Ryan, Douglass Ullman, John Pascoe, Raul Diaz, and John Chessare. (1986). "Maternal Social Support as a Predictor of Mother-Child Stress and Stimulation." *Child Abuse and Neglect*, vol. 10.

Allen, Charlotte Vale. (1980). *Daddy's Girl*, New York: Wyndhambooks.

Althusser, Louis. (1972). "Ideology and Ideological State Apparatuses." *Lenin and Philosophy and Other Essays* New York: Monthly Review Press.

Anthias, Floya and Nira Yuval-Davis. (1992). *Racialized Boundaries: Race, Nation, Gender, Colour and Class and the Anti-racist Struggle*. London: Routledge.

Aries, Philippe. (1962). *Centuries of Childhood: A Social History of Family Life*. New York: Vintage Books.

Atkinson, Paul. (1990). *The Ethnographic Imagination: Textual Constructions of Reality*. London: Routledge.

Ayoub, Catherine and Marion Jacewitz. (1982). "Families at Risk of Poor Parenting: A Descriptive Study of Sixty at-Risk Families in a Model Prevention Program." *Child Abuse and Neglect*, vol. 6.

Badgley, Robin. (1984). *The Report of the Committee on Sexual Offenses Against Children and Youths*. Ottawa: Health and Welfare Canada.

Bagley, Chris. (1982). "Child Sexual Abuse: A Child Welfare Perspective." In Kenneth L. Levitt and Brian Wharf (eds.), *The Challenge of Child Welfare*. Vancouver: University of British Columbia Press.

Bala, N.C. (1987). *Review of Child Abuse Register*. Kingston: Queen's University.

Bertaux, Daniel and Paul Thompson. (1992). *Between Generations: Family Models, Myths, and Memories*. New York: Oxford University Press.

Baker, Maureen. (1988). "Child Abuse." *Current Issue Review*. Ottawa: Library of Parliament.

Begin, Patricia. (1992). "Child Abuse." *Current Issue Review*. Ottawa: Library of Canada.

Bell, Vikki. (1993). "Governing Childhood: Neo-Liberalism and the Law." *Economy and Society*, vol. 22, no. 3.

Beltiame, Julian. (1995). "Is Attack on Welfare Moms a Legitimate Social Venture?" *Vancouver Sun*, March 11, 1995, pp.A16-17.

Bentovim, Aaron, *et al.* (1988). *Child Sexual Abuse Within the Family: Assessment and Treatment, the Work of the Great Ormond Street Sexual Abuse Team.* Toronto: Wright.

Bernstein, J.M. (1991). "Grand Narratives." In David Wood (ed.), *On Paul Ricoeur.* London: Routledge.

Bird, G. and M. Sporakowski. (1994). *Taking Sides. Clashing Views on Controversial Issues In Family and Personal Relationships.* Connecticut: Dushkin.

Bowman, Ted. (1993). "The Father-Son Project." *Journal of Contemporary Human Services*, vol. 74, no. 1.

Bradbury, Bettina. (1992). *Canadian Family History*, Toronto: Copp Clark Pitman Ltd.

Brender, William, Robin Gagnon, & Elaine Dubrow. (undated). *Child Sexual Abuse: Risk Factors for Negative Long-Term Effects.* Ottawa: Family Violence Prevention Division of Health Canada.

British Columbia Task Force on Family Violence. (1992). *Is Anyone Listening?* Victoria, B.C.: Ministry of Women's Equality.

Bronstein, Phyllis. (1988). "Marital and Parenting Roles in Transition." In P. Bronstein (ed.), *Fatherhood Today: Men's Changing Role in the Family.* New York:John Wiley and Sons.

Brooks, Richard. (1996). "Paedophile Fears Kill Greenpeace Advert." *The Observer*, June 30, 1996, p. 8.

Butler-Sloss, Elizabeth. (1988). *Report of the Inquiry into Child Abuse in Cleveland 1987.* London.

Callahan, Marilyn. (1993). "The Administrative and Practical Context: Perspectives From the Front Line." In Brian Wharf (ed.), *Rethinking Child Welfare In Canada.* Toronto: McClelland and Stewart.

Campbell, Beatrix. (1988.). *Unofficial Secrets. Child Sexual Abuse: The Cleveland Case.* London: Virago.

Chalin, C. and M. Lewittes (1988). *Medical Assessment, Treatment, and Follow-up of Sexually Abused Children: A Review of the Literature.* Ottawa: Health and Welfare Canada.

Children's Aid Society of the City of Sarnia and County of Lambton (1982). Judicial Review into the Care of Kim Ann Poppen.

Children's Services Division of the Ontario Ministry of Community and Social
Services. (1981). *Consultation Paper.*

Cohen, Anthony (1993). "Boundaries of Consciousness and Consciousness of Boundaries." *Presentation, Amsterdam Conference on Critical Thinking in the Anthropology of Ethnicity.*

Cohen, Judith A. and Anthony P. Mannarino. (1991). "Incest." In Robert T. Ammerman and Michael Hersen (eds.), *Case Studies in Family Violence.* New York: Plenum Press.

Cohn, A. Finkelhor, D. and C. Holmes. (1985). "Preventing Adults from Becoming Child Sex Molestors." *Working Papers 25*, Chicago National Committee for the Prevention of Child Abuse.

Connell, R.W. (1987). *Gender and Power.* London: Polity Press.

Commission de protection des droits de la jeunesse. (1993). *Rapport Annuel.* Québec: Les publications du Québec.

Community Panel Family and Childrens' Services Legislation Review in British Columbia. (October 1992). *Making Changes: A Place to Start.* Victoria: Ministry of Social Services.

Cousins, M. and A. Hussain. (1984). *Michel Foucault.* London: MacMillan.

Currie, David, W. (1988). *The Abusive Husband: An Approach to Intervention.* Toronto: Clarke Institute of Psychiatry.

Dale, Peter, Murray Davies, Tony Morrison and Jim Waters. (1986). *Dangerous Families.* London: Tavistock.

Dally, Ann. (1982). *Inventing Motherhood: The Consequences of an Ideal.* London: Burnett Books.

de Certeau, Michel. (1988). *The Practice of Everyday Life.* Berkeley: University of California Press.

Dawson, Ross. (1982). *Sexual Abuse of Children. A Training Programme for Children's Aid Society Staff.* Ontario: Ministry of Community and Social Services.

Denzin, Norman. (1989. *Interpretive Interactionism.* Newbury Park: Sage.

Dingwall, Robert. (1989). "Some Problems About Predicting Child Abuse and Neglect." In Olive Stevenson (ed.), *Child Abuse: Professional Practice and Public Policy.* London: Harvester Wheatsheaf.

Donzelot, Jacques. (1979). *Policing of Families: Welfare Versus the State.* London: Hutchinson.

Dreyfus, H. and P. Rabinow. (1983). *Michel Foucault: Beyond Structuralism and Hermeneutics*. Chicago: University of Chicago Press.

Eade, Dr. (1981). *Proceedings of the Working Conference on Preventive Strategies in Child Abuse*. Toronto.

Eichler, Margrit. (1988). *Families in Canada Today: Recent Changes and their Policy Consequences*, 2nd ed. Toronto: Gage.

Ethier, Louise S., Carl Lacharité, and Germain Couture. (1995). "Childhood Adversity, Parental Stress, and Depression of Negligent Mothers." *Child Abuse and Neglect*, vol 19, no.5.

Fasick, Frank. (1989). "Socialization Beyond Childhood." In K. Ishwaran (ed.), *Family and Marriage*. Toronto: Wall and Thompson.

Federal-Provincial Working Group on Child and Family Services Information. (1994). *Child Welfare in Canada: The Role of Provincial and Territorial Authorities in Cases of Child Abuse*. Ottawa: Supply and Services Canada.

Ferrato, Donna. (1991). *Living With The Enemy*. New York: Aperture.

Fine, Sean. (1991). "Sex abuse by women ignored, psychologist tells conference." *Globe and Mail*, October 30, 1991, A1.

Finkelhor, D. (1979). *Sexually Victimised Children*. New York: Free Press.

Foucault, Michel. (1977). *Discipline and Punish: The Birth of the Prison*. London: Penguin Books.

Foucault, Michel. (1980). *The History of Sexuality: Volume 1: An Introduction*. New York: Vintage Books.

Foucault, Michel. (1983). *The Archeology of Knowledge*. London: Tavistock.

Fox, Bonnie, (ed.) (1988). *Family Bonds and Gender Divisions*. Toronto: Canadian Scholar's Press Inc.

Fox, Bonnie, (ed.) (1993). *Family Patterns and Gender Relations*. Oxford: O.U.P.

Freeman, Mark. (1993). *Rewriting the Self. History, Memory, Narrative*. London: Routledge.

Franklin, Clyde W. (1984). *The Changing Definition of Masculinity*. London: Plenum Press.

Fraser, Sylvia. (1988). *My Father's House: A Memoir of Incest and of Healing*. Don Mills, Ontario: Collins Paperbacks.

Garbarino, James. (1993). "Reinventing Fatherhood." *Journal of Contemporary Human Services*, Vol.74, no. 1.

Gardner, Richard, A. (1987). *Sex Abuse Legitimacy Scale*. Cresskill, New [201]
Jersey: Creative Therapeutics.

Gelles, R. and M. Strauss. (1988). *Intimate Violence*, New York: Simon and
Schuster cited Volpe, Richard (1989).*Poverty and Child Abuse* Toronto:
Institute for the Prevention of Child Abuse.

Giaretto, Henry. (1982). "A Comprehensive Child Sexual Abuse Treatment
Program." *Child Abuse and Neglect*, vol. 6.

Ginsburg, Ruth (1991). "The Anxiety of Fatherhood." *Modern Language
Quarterly*, vol. 52, no. 4.

Government of Canada. (1992). *Family Violence in Canada: A Call to Action*.
Ottawa: Ministry of Supply and Services.

Gray, Jane, Christy Cutler, Janet Dean, Henry C. Kempe. (1976). "Perinatal
Assessment of Mother-Baby Interaction." In R.E. Helfer & C.H. Kempe
(eds.), *Child Abuse and Neglect: The Family and the Community*.
Cambridge, Mass.: Ballinger.

Gray, Jane, *et al.* (1982). *Welcome Baby Manual*. Unpublished version, files of
the Institute for the Prevention of Child Abuse, Toronto.

Greenland, Cyril (1978). *Child Abuse Deaths in Ontario*. Ontario Ministry of
Communication and Social Services.

Health Canada. (1993). *Four Variations of Family Violence: A Review of
Sociological Research*. Ottawa: National Clearing House on Family
Violence.

Hearn, Jeff. (1990). "Child Abuse and Men's Violence." In The Violence
Against Children Study Group. *Taking Child Abuse Seriously*. London:
Unwin Hyman.

Hechtman, Lily. (1989). "Teenage Mothers and Their Children: Risk and
Problems: A Review." *Canadian Journal of Psychiatry 34*.

Herbert, Carol. (1987). "Expert Medical Assessment in Determining
Probability of Alleged Child Sexual Abuse." *Child Abuse and Neglect*, vol.
11.

Hercules, Trevor. (1989). *Labelled a Black Villain*. London:Fourth Estate
Limited.

Hite, Shere. (1994). *The Hite Report on the Family; Growing Up Under
Patriarchy*. London: Hodder and Stoughton.

Hoff, Lee Ann. (1990). *Battered Women as Survivors*. London:Routledge.

Hooper, Carol-Ann. (1992). "Child Sexual Abuse and the Regulation of Women: Variations on a Theme." In Carol Smart (ed.), *Regulating Womanhood*. London: Routledge.

Hustak, Alan. (1995). "Children Who Kill." *Montreal Gazette*, April 8, B8.

Institute for the Prevention of Child Abuse. (1990). Conference Paper, Toronto.

Ishwaran, K. (1989). *Family and Marriage*. Toronto: Wall and Thompson.

Jackson, Brian. (1984). *Fatherhood*. London: George Allen & Unwin.

James, Allison and Alan Prout. (1990). *Constructing and Reconstructing Childhood: Contemporary Issues in the Sociological Study of Childhood*. Hampshire: The Falmer Press.

Journal of Canadian Women's Studies. (1989). vol. 10, nos 2 & 3.

Justice, R. and R. Justice. (1976). *The Abusing Family*. New York: Human Sciences Press.

Kaplan, Ann, E. (1992). *Motherhood and Representation*. London: Routledge.

Kendall-Tackett, K. and A. Simon. (1987). "Perpetrators and Their Acts: Data from 365 Adults Molested as Children." *Journal of Child Abuse and Neglect 11*.

Kenny, Michael. (1994). "Memories of Child Sexual Abuse," unpublished paper.

Knowles, Caroline. (1990). "Black Families and Social Services." In A. Cambridge and S. Feuchtwang (eds.), *Antiracist Strategies*. Aldershot, England: Avery.

Knowles, Caroline. (1991). *Medical Intervention in the Management of Child Abuse in Canada*. LaMarsh Research Programme Report #42. Toronto: York University.

Knowles, Caroline. (1992). *Race, Discourse and Labourism*. London: Routledge.

Knowles, C. and S. Mercer. (1992). "Feminism and Antiracism: An Exploration of the Political Possibilities." In J. Donald and A. Rattansi (eds.), *Race, Culture and Difference*. London: Sage.

Knowles, Caroline. (1994)."Biographical Explorations of Blackness and Schizophrenia." *Lives and Works. Auto/Biography, 3:1 & 3:2*

Korbin, Jill. (1987). "Incarcerated Mothers' Perceptions and Interpretations of their Fatally Maltreated Children." *Child Abuse and Neglect*, vol. 11.

Kotch, J.B. and Thomas L. Parke. (1986). "Family and Social Factors Associated with Substantiation of Child Abuse and Neglect Reports." *Journal of Family Violence*, vol. 1, no. 2.

Kuypers, Joseph, A. (1992). *Man's Will to Hurt: Investigating the Causes, Supports and Varieties of His Violence*. Halifax: Fernwood Publishing.

Laing, R.D. and A. Esterton. (1964). *Sanity, Madness and the Family*, New York: Basic Books.

Lamb, Michael. (1983). "Fatherhood and Social Policy in International Perspective: An Introduction." In Michael Lamb and Abraham Sagi (eds.), *Fatherhood and Family Policy*. London: Lawrence Erlbaum Associates.

Langley, Roger and Richard C. Levy. (1977). *Wife Beating: The Silent Crisis*. New York: E.P. Dutton.

Lauer, Jeanette and Robert Lauer. (1994). *Marriage and Family: The Quest for Intimacy*. Madison, Wisconsin: Brown and Benchmark Publishers.

Ledger, Karen and Daphne Williams. (1981). *Parents at Risk: An Instructional Programme for Perinatal Assessment and Preventive Information* . Victoria, Province of British Columbia: Ministry of Health.

Leventhal, John, Kathleen Fearn, and Carol Stashwick. (1986). "Clinical Data Used by Pediatric Residents to Assess Parenting." *Child Abuse and Neglect Vol.10*.

Levine, James, A. (1993). "Involving Fathers in Head Start: A Framework for Public Policy and Program Development." *Journal of Contemporary Human Services*, vol. 74, no. 1.

Lovett, Beverly, B. (1995). "Child Sexual Abuse: The Female Victim's Relationship with her Non-Offending Mother." *Child Abuse and Neglect*, vol. 19, no. 6.

Macey, David. (1993). *The Lives of Michel Foucault*. London: Hutchinson.

Mackie, Marlene. (1993). "Primary Socialization in Cross Cultural Context." In G.N. Ramu (ed.), *Marriage and the Family in Canada Today*. Scarborough: Prentice Hall.

Martin, Marjorie. (1985). "Poverty and Child Welfare." In Kenneth L. Levitt and Brian Wharf (eds.), *The Challenge of Child Welfare*. Vancouver: University of British Columbia Press.

McAdoo, John, L. (1988). "Changing perspectives on the Role of the Black Father." In Phyllis Bronstein and Carolyn Pape Cowan (eds.), *Fatherhood Today: Men's Changing Role in the Family*. New York: John Wiley & Sons.

[204]   McAdoo, John, L. (1993). *The Role of African-American Fathers: An Ecological Perspective*. The Journal of Contemporary Human Services, vol. 74, no. 1.

McGregor, B. and D. Dutton. (1988). "Child Sexual Abuse Within Populations that Require Health System Intervention: What is Known About its Prevalence and Service Costs?" Ottawa: Health and Welfare Canada.

McKee, Lorna and Margaret O'Brien. (1982). "The Father Figure: Some Current Orientations and Historical Perspectives." In L. McKee and M. O'Brien (eds.), *The Father Figure*, London: Tavistock.

McLaren, Angus. (1990). *Our Own Master Race: Eugenics in Canada, 1885-1945*. Toronto: McClelland and Stewart Limited.

Mian, Dr. (1990). Interview conducted at Sick Children's Hospital, Toronto.

Miller, Alice. (1987). *For Your Own Good: The Roots of Violence in Child Rearing*. London: Virago.

Monsebraaten, Laurie. (1995). "Welfare's Bogeywomen." *Toronto Star*, August 12, 1995, pp. C1, C4.

Montreal Childrens' Hospital (1988). "Epidemiology of Risk Factors in Family Violence."

Montreal Gazette, 26 and 27 May 1995.

Morgan, David. (1992). *Discovering Men*. London: Routledge.

Morrison, Blake. (1993). *And When Did You Last See Your Father?* London: Granta Books.

Nathanson, Constance. (1991). Dangerous Passage. *The Social Control of Sexuality in Women's Adolescence*. Philadelphia: Temple University Press.

Nicholson, Nigel. (1992). *Vita and Harold*. The Letters of Vita Sackville-West and Harold Nicolson. New York: Putnams and Sons.

North West Territories Native Women's Association and Social Services Department (1989).

Paré, Jean. (1994). "La famille dans tous ses états." *L'Actualité*, July 1994, pp.22-24.

Parent and Child Therapy Society, The. (1984). "Learning and Teaching in Child Abuse." Health and Welfare Canada.

Parsons, Talcott & Bales. (1955). *Family, Socialization and Interaction Process*. Toronto: Collier McMillan.

Parton, Nigel (1985). *The Politics of Child Abuse*. MacMillan

Parton, Christine and Nigel Parton. (1989). "Child Protection, the Law and [*205*]
Dangerousness." In Olive Stevenson (ed.), *Child Abuse: Professional
Practice and Public Policy*. London: Harvester Wheatsheaf.

Petersen, Betty. (1991). *Dancing with Daddy: A Childhood Lost and a Life
Regained*. Toronto: Bantam Books.

Phoenix, A., A. Woollett and E. Lloyd. (1991). *Motherhood: Meanings,
Practices and Ideologies*. London: Sage.

Pruett, Kyle, D. (1993). "The Paternal Presence." *The Journal of
Contemporary Human Services*, vol. 74, no. 1.

Rae-Grant, Dr. (1981). *Proceedings of the Working Conference on Preventive
Strategies in Child Abuse*. Toronto.

Rainwater, Lee. (1970). *Behind Ghetto Walls: Black Families in a Federal Slum*.
Chicago: Aldine Publishing Company.

Ramazanoglou, Caroline. (1992). "Feminism and Liberation." In L. McDowell
and R. Pringle (eds), *Defining Women*. London: Polity Press.

Ramu, G.N. (ed.) (1993). *Marriage and the Family in Canada Today*.
Scarborough, Ont.: Prentice Hall.

Report of the Gove inquiry into Child Protection (B.C.).(1995). *Matthew's
Story*. B.C.: Ministry of Social Services.

Report of the Special Advisor to the Minister of National Health and Welfare
on Child Sexual Abuse in Canada. (1991). *Reaching For Solutions*. Ottawa:
Ministry of Supply and Services.

Rice, Philip, E. (1993). *Intimate Relationships, Marriage and Families*.
Mountain View, California: Mayfield Publishing Company.

Ricoeur, Paul (1991). "Life in Quest of Narrative." In D. Wood (ed.), *On Paul
Ricoeur: Narrative and Interpretation*. London: Routledge.

Riley, Denise. (1983). *War in the Nursery*. London: Virago.

Rose, Nikolas. (1989). *Governing the Soul: The Shaping of the Private Self*.
London: Routledge.

Rutter, Michael. (1984). *Maternal Deprivation Reassessed*. New York: Penguin
Books.

Rustin, M. and M. Rustin. (1987). *Narratives of Love and Loss*. London:
Verso.

Sandelowski, Margaret. (1994). "Separate but Equal. Fetal Ultrasonography
and the Transformation of Expectant Mother/Fatherhood." *Gender and
Society*, vol. 8, no. 2.

[206]   Sawula, Silva. (1989). *Physical and Sexual Abuse Assessment Guides*. Toronto: The Institute for the Prevention of Child Abuse.

Saxton, Lloyd. (1993). *The Individual, Marriage and the Family*. Belmont, California: Wadsworth Publishing Company.

Schindler, F. and H. Arkowitz. (1986). "The Assessment of Mother-Child Interactions in Physically Abusive and Nonabusive Families." *Journal of Family Violence*, vol. 1, no. 3.

Schorr, Lisbeth (1991). "Children, Families and the Cycle of Disadvantage." *Canadian Journal of Psychiatry*, vol. 36.

Seagull, Elizabeth. (1987). "Social Support and Child Maltreatment: A Review of the Evidence." *Child Abuse and Neglect*, vol. 11.

Sereny, Gitta. (1994). "A Child Murderer." *Independent on Sunday*, April 23, 1995, pp. 8-12.

Shaffron, Rona and Sheila Baslaw. (1980). *Families for Families. Ottawa-Carleton Child Abuse Demonstration Project*. Ontario: Ministry of Community and Social Services.

Sigurdson, Eric and Grant Reid. (1987). *External Review into Matters Relating to the System of Dealing with Child Abuse in Winnipeg*. Manitoba: Ministry of Community Services.

Smart, Carol. (1992). *Regulating Womanhood*. London: Routledge.

Smith, Dorothy. (1987). *The Everyday World as Problematic*. Toronto: University of Toronto Press.

Stacey, Judith. (1993). "Brave New Families in the Second North American Family Revolution." *Transition*. Ottawa: Vanier Institute of the Family.

Stanley, Liz. (1992). "Process in Feminist Biography and Feminist Epistemology." In Teresa Iles (ed.), *All Sides of the Subject: Women and Biography*. New York: Teacher's College Press.

Stanley, Liz. (1993). "On Auto/Biography in Sociology." In *Sociology*, vol. 27, no. 1, pp.41-52.

Steen, Edward. (1990). "Has child sex reached the age of consent?" *The Independent on Sunday*, Nov. 18, 1990, p.5.

Strand, Virginia C. (1991). "Mid-Phase Treatment with Mothers in Incest Families." *Clinical Social Work Journal*, vol. 19, no. 4.

Strong, Bryan and Christine DeVault. (1992). *The Marriage and Family Experience*. St. Paul, Minn.: West Publishing Co.

Turner, Jay. (1982). *Risk and Prevention for Maladaptive Parenting*. London, [207]
Ont.: The University of Western Ontario.

Ursel, Jane. (1992). *Private Lives, Public Policy: 100 Years of State Intervention in the Family*. Toronto: Women's Press.

Vale, Edward. (1989). *Relationships Between Spousal Violence and the Physical Abuse of Children*. Toronto: The Institute for the Prevention of Child Abuse.

Valpy, Michael. (1996). "Taking it out on Child Care." *Globe and Mail*, 24 January, 1996.

Valverde, M. (1992). "Representing Childhood: The Multiple Fathers of the Dionne Quintuplets." In C. Smart *Regulating Womanhood*. London: Routledge.

Vanier Institute for the Family. (1994). *Transition*.

Violence Against Children Study Group. (1990). *Taking Child Abuse Seriously*. London: Unwin Hyman.

Vobejda, Barbara. (1996). "Clinton Sets Teen Welfare Standards." *Guardian Weekly*, May 12, 1996, p.16.

Volpe, Richard. (1989). *Poverty and Child Abuse*. Toronto: Institute for the Prevention of Child Abuse.

Ward, Margaret. (1994). *The Family Dynamic: A Canadian Perspective*. Scarborough, Ont: Nelson.

Wash, Gayle and Carmen Knudson-Martin. (1994). "Gender Identity and Family Relationships: Perspectives from Incestuous Fathers." *Contemporary Family Therapy*, vol. 15, no. 5.

Webber, Marlene. (1991). *Street Kids: The Tragedy of Canada's Runaways*. Toronto: The University of Toronto Press.

Weeks, Jeffrey. (1986). *Sexuality*. Chichester: Ellis Horwood.

White, Hayden. (1991). "The Metaphysics of Narrativity." In David Wood (ed.), *On Paul Ricoeur*. London: Routledge.

Winnicott, D.W. (1991). *The Child, the Family and the Outside World*. London: Penguin Books.

Wolfe, David (1985). "Child-Abusive Parents: An Empirical Review and Analysis." *Public Family Violence Prevention Division & Psychiatric Bulletin*. Ottawa: Health and Welfare Canada.

[208]   Wolfe, David. (1989). *Child Abusive Parents: An Empirical Review and Analysis*. Ottawa: Health and Welfare Canada.

Wolfe, David. (1990). Institute for the Prevention of Child Abuse, Conference Presentation, Toronto.

Woodhead, Martin. (1990). "Psychology and the Cultural Construction of Children's Needs." Allison James and Alan Prout (eds.), *Constructing and Reconstructing Childhood: Contemporary Issues in the Social Study of Childhood*. London: Falmer Press.

Woodling, B.A. *et al.* (1986). "The Use of Colposcope in the Diagnosis of Sexual Abuse in the Pediatric Age Group." *Journal of Child Abuse and Neglect 10*.

Wynne, Jane. (1989). "Medical Aspects of Child Abuse." In Allan Levy (ed.), *Focus on Child Abuse: Medical and Legal Social Work Perspectives*. London: Hawksmere.

INDEX